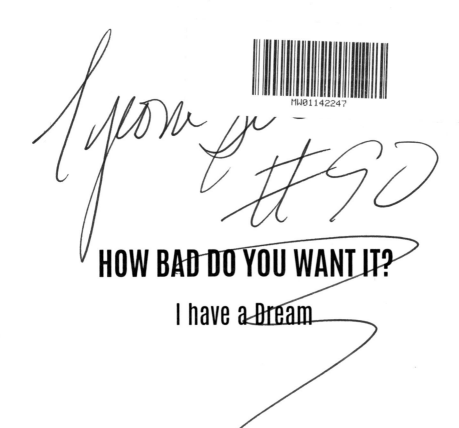

HOW BAD DO YOU WANT IT?

I have a Dream

Pastor Tyronne Stowe

PRESS

Scripture quotations taken from the American Standard Version (ASV)- *public domain.*

Scripture quotations taken from the The Holy Bible, New International Version (NIV). Copyright © 1973, 1978, 1984, 2011 by Biblica, Inc.™. Used by permission. All rights reserved.

www.xulonpress.com

INTRODUCTION:

How Bad Do You Want It!

This book is dedicated to all the people in the world that have had enough of mediocrity. People that refuse to settle for social complacency as their destiny! People that know there is more to them than what people perceive. People that refuse to be labeled and stereo typed as average. People that have been overlooked as ordinary instead of extra ordinary! If you are reading this book, its proof that you know that you haven't tapped into your greatest potential yet. God is not through with you yet, the best is still yet to come and God is going to do big things through you!

As you read this book, my prayer is that your self-confidence and God's plan for your life, will leap into reality! All the gifts and talents of possibilities will be stirred and released inside of you. This book was written for those, like myself, who needed just a little more coaching.

A personal trainer who knows that your life is different from everyone else's. The journey you are about to take is life altering. All you need is a little more inspiration, and a partner to run with it! The Bible says in Ecclesiastes 4:9 that "two are better than one, because they have a good reward for their labor." The reward is if there is a problem, a lack of motivation or discouragement, or failure then if one falls, the other person is there to lift the other up out the ditch of defeat or doubt; but woe to him that is alone when he falleth, and hath not another to lift him up.

I want to be that person to help you reach your full potential! I want to lift you out of any fall that life has dealt you. I want to remind you that God has lifted you up to be seated in Heavenly Places! I trust that we can be open to each other. I want you to express your inner thoughts, fears, dislikes, disappointments, discouragements, your perceptions and other issues that have left a bad taste in your mouth. I ask you to be truthful to yourself and make an honest assessment about yourself as we travel the road to victory. In the past, you have been close to success, close to landing that dream job having money in the bank, a beautiful home, a wonderful marriage, a great career, traveling, a great family, loving friends, and it's all yours for the taking!

It's all a matter of, How Bad Do You Want It?

Chapter 1

YOUR NEW DESTINY

I want to encourage you, that it is never too late. God can do it for you! You are not crazy, and you have a self- portrait, an image of yourself that is real, it's tangible but you have not lived it yet. The best is still yet to come for you. God has promised you something and has shown you something and we can go after it. This is the new lifestyle you will live to bring glory to God! This picture is the vision in the future of how things will be. It's a snap shot of what's waiting for you. But how bad do I want you to get there? How do I bring it to pass for you? This Vision you are carrying is the end product, and we haven't made it to the end yet. There is a winner in you, and a champion inside of you! But it must be developed first. You must be seasoned and matured to handle the blessings that are on the way.

We must grow up to be more than conquerors. Romans 8:37 "In all these things we are more than conquerors through him who loved us." The feelings you have are right, your image of how things should be is correct, but your present situation isn't measuring up. There is a screaming voice of pain and frustration inside of you that must be silenced by success. I know what you are going through all too well; the pain of knowing you were called to be but living around life. Sometimes we are surrounded by family and friends that didn't know who you where or what God has called you to do, which is a challenging dilemma. We allowed them to define us, nickname us, scare us and conform us into being someone else. The devil is a liar! Together we will be who God has called us to be, and we will see the fulfillment of all God has shown you! Don't get weary in well doing for in due season. Galatians 6:9 "Let us not grow weary while doing good, for in due season we shall reap if we do not lose heart" I just want you to know my friend this is your season! I don't believe you heard me! This is your season! You will reap, if you faint not, do not faint my friend, be patient God will bring it all to pass for you! Proverbs 24:10 "If you falter in a time of trouble, how small is your strength." There is nothing small about you when you tap into God's plan for your life!

Little is much when you put it in the master hands, your strength is your ability to trust in God! You must trust God in every circumstance. Our little act of faith will yield great blessing to all around you. You are blessed to be a blessing to each other, just put you little in the Master's hands.

In Matt 14:15-21 there is a great story to highlight this fact that little is much in the Master's hand! Jesus went to a desolate place. He went to a place of lack. He chose a dry place where nothing could grow. And I believe that Jesus chose this place, to use as a life lesson. That faith in Him will overcome ever lacking necessity that you have in your life. As Jesus taught the word of God, it got late and the disciples told the people to go send the crowds away, that they may get something to eat. But Jesus said, don't send them away, it took us to long to come together, my word says come unto me and I will give you rest!

Jesus said, you give them something to eat. They went through the crowds and only found two fish and five loaves of bread.

Jesus said bring it to me! Jesus will cause it to be pressed down and running over men will give unto our bosom!

Whatever you have people of God, we have to learn to bring it to Jesus. He will supply our every need!

Jesus ordered the people to sit down on the grass, He took the two fish and the five loaves and looked up into heaven, and He blessed the food and the loaves. Then He gave it to His Disciples, and the Disciples gave them to the crowd and they all ate, I said they all ate and were satisfied. God will supply our every need according to His riches in Glory by Christ Jesus! God's riches are for the believer today. Stop holding back the blessings God has in stored for you, just put it all in His hands. You will be satisfied, you will have more than enough, and not enough. The Bible goes on to say, they picked up 12 full baskets of left overs. There was in the crowd's five thousand men who ate, and there are twice as many women in the world than men, so it could have been at least 10,000 women there too and most people have at least two children equaling another 10,000 children.

When the boy offered his offering, and put it into the hand of Jesus. It multiplied and caused increase and the miracle of that day, over 25,000 souls were feed and there were still 12 basket of left overs. Just put whatever you have into the hands of the Lord. Little is much in the Master's hands! God would have us all to know that our little efforts in Life can go a long way, just put it all in His hands

Our strength is our willingness to believe in God, and our beliefs must increase. Our belief in what God said, and what God has shown you must be stronger than any doubts. Most people want a lot out of life, but very few ever actually receive what they set out to accomplish. People give up on themselves and they give up on God. Can I tell you that God hasn't given up on you, so why have you given up on him?

Chapter 2

ARE YOU A QUITTER?

I want to ask you something, are you a quitter? A quitter means one who gives up and stops pursuing the purpose that they were ordained to do. I want to tell you a story of the world's greatest quitter, his name was Judas. The name Judas is derived from the word to celebrate. Determine today not to quit, determine today not to be a Judas and live to see the fullness of your life and be celebrated. Most of us have settled for a life that was not designed by God. That is why it is time for us to change and take the steps of faith necessary towards a victorious way of living. I want to tell you a story of a man that made great strides in his life and finished strong, it is not how you start but how you finish. Your former reign shall not be worthy to be compared to you later reign. Haggai 2:9 – "The latter glory of this house will be greater than the former,' says the LORD of hosts, 'and in this place I will give peace,' declares the LORD of hosts." You will have peace in this new life and character of greatness.

1 Chronicles 4:9-10 "There was a young man named Jabez. Jabez was more honorable than his brothers. God is going to do it for you because we are honest enough to except our weakness and flaws. You are honest enough to know that we need help from on High. God is

going to show himself strong to us. Yet His mother named him Jabez saying, "Because I bore *him* with pain." His mother was in pain and she named him pain. Every time she called him she would remember the trauma as though it was today. Every time she saw him, the pains of the past would come into reality. Just think what would Jabez life be like if his mother would have named him, beautiful or wonderful?

Now Jabez called on the God of Israel, and took a chance to put his trust in God to change the course of his life. Jabez said, "oh that you would bless me indeed and enlarge my border, and that your hand might be with me, and that you would keep *me* from harm that *it* may not pain me!" God granted Jabez what he requested. I want you to take a chance and trust God, he will grant your request.

Expect great things to happen in your life. Dream big dreams and believe that you will see the fulfillment of them, and stop settling for less. Go against the odds and shoot for the stars. Someone is going to shine, why not you? You're loaded with gifts, talents and abilities, love yourself enough to let them come out. There is a new life awaiting you, take a step of faith today out of mediocrity and you are one step closer to your new reality. Fight within yourself and refuse to be satisfied with the limits placed on you today.

God's best is waiting for you. Know that the notion you have inside of you is for better and abundance is of God. It's a Kingdom Impulse, pushing you to trust God and be who he called you to be. Most of us have settled for a life that God has not designed. We have allowed the world to architect us a life of defeat and depression. I come to inform you that those days are over and a new day is dawning in your life. My assignment is to awaken the sleeping giant of greatness inside of you. The alarm clock has sounded, now is the time for you to get up and get out of the bed of defeat. How bad do you want it?

Chapter 3

HOW BIG IS YOUR DREAM?

Can you remember as a child, how you use to dream and play make-believe? Do you remember day dreaming, and a big smile would come on your face? Dreams have a purpose, dreams let you know what's possible. Dreams can come true; yes, and they can happen to you! What is your dream? Dreams are visions of how things could be or a snap shot of what could be. Your dream is a footprint to follow. Dreams let you know what's capable of happening. You can live your dream. How bad do you want it?

Dream definition:

A dream is a succession of involuntary images, thoughts or emotions passing through the brain. Everything in life that has ever been invented, discovered, written or created all started with a thought passing through the brain. This was the beginning stages of dream animation.

The brain is the canvas of art; pictures manifest of what is possible. The brain is where reality is conceived. If you can think it, you can achieve it!

But how is your thinking?

The world would like for you to think that you can't achieve your goals and dreams. You must think that you were born to succeed in everything you put your hands onto! Proverbs 23:7 For as he thinks within himself so is he!

Or a snap shot of what could be? I have learned that positive thinking is an art. We are told by the Bible to think of things that are above, the art is to keep your mind on heavenly things and not on earthly things Colossians 3:2 In the book of Job there is a great story of the power of negative vs positive thinking. We need to learn from this lesson taught from the Bible in the book of Job. Job focused all his attention on what he didn't want to happen and Job was afraid for his children. Job thought that his children would sin against God and the penalty would be death. Job's daily thoughts were of his children's sins, which caused him to worry every day and sacrifice every day. Job invested his time in negative thinking and it produced a bad event. This means we must keep our mind on things that matter.

Job had a big family 7 sons and three daughters Job had great possessions sheep, camels, yoke of oxen, donkeys, and very many servants; Job was the greatest men of the east.

Job would send and consecrate them, rising up early in the morning and offering burnt offerings *according to* the number of them all; for Job said, "Perhaps my sons have sinned and cursed God in their hearts." Thus Job did continually.

I like to say, that Job was worrying about His children and them sinning against God. But Job never is found holding His Children accountable.

Job's thinking every day could have attributed to his children dying. Every day he thought negatively about his children's lifestyle.

Job's thinking on what he didn't want gave life to make it happen.

While he was still speaking, another also came and said, "Your sons and your daughters were eating and drinking wine in their oldest brother's house, and behold, a great wind came from across the wilderness and struck the four corners of the house, and it fell on the young people and they died, and I alone have escaped to tell you." Job 3:25

For the thing which I greatly feared is come upon me, and that which I was afraid of is come unto me.

Concentration and focus is a must. Our thinking is vitally important to our state of mind. Our state of mind is reflective to our state of being. You have to think right to life right. As you grow stronger in every area of life. If you don't mine, it doesn't matter! This means we must keep the mind on things that matter. Most of our valuable time is being wasted on things that don't matter or unwanted challenges. When things don't matter put them out of you mind.

It is so easy to be distracted from what we really want and we must learn to think on the things we want. When you have a dream, a thought and a vison you must think it through and live what you saw. Break the limits off your life.

Nehemiah understood this principle when he stated in Nehemiah 6: 3 I'm doing a great work, I can't come down. Why shall the work cease?- what should take months came to past in record time of 52 days. Focus yourself to the mission completion and perfection is yours. Let's go to work on your vision.

How is your vision?

You need to see your vision to be in it. If you can see your vision, you can achieve it! If you can believe it, you can receive it! You can achieve it! How bad do you want it? Know that if you can dream it, you can achieve it! Philippians 4:13 "I can do all things through Christ, who gives me strength." How bad do you want it?

I have a question to ask? Are you a believer? Yes, you are a believer not a doubter! What do you believe? Ephesians 3:20 "Now to him who is able to do immeasurably more than all we ask or imagine according to his power that is at work within us." There is power and potential inside of you, but will you let God bring it out of you? Will you leave your mark in the world that you have been here?

Genesis 7:1 God said Noah, "go into the ark, you and your whole family because I have found you righteous in this generation." What will God say about your life? What are you building? Build a life that Pleases God! Do you believe in you? Do you believe in your dream? Most people have more confidence in someone else, then in themselves. Do you believe and trust in yourself? Do you love your-self? These are really honest questions that need to be pondered and answered by you. Because being a dream chaser, will push you in tight places where you don't want to be but is necessary for you to qualify for dream satisfaction!

One of the greatest men in my lifetime had a dream, we all know him as the late, great Reverend Dr. Martin Luther King! He spoke of having a dream and his dream cost him his life! Your dream will also require determination, discipline, and possibly death to see the dream manifest! Do you have a dream? Yes, I know you do, but what is the dream? Write your dream down and make it plain for others to run with it! Have you shared the Dream with others? No? Why not? They must know the dream and visions to help bring your dream to pass! Stating the dream, concretes the dream and helps reaffirm your belief too. Stop suppressing the dream release it to the angels to bring it to pass and fill your atmosphere with faith! Hebrews 11:1 "Now faith is confidence in what we hope for and assurance about what we do not see." As you speak your dreams and visions, little substances will appear before your eyes! You will see incredible resources surprisingly produce itself as a result of you dream speaking.

Dr. King was very vocal about his dream. He shared his dream with masses of people and in return he received a massive response. Others will be ordained to help you in your struggle, and will come from all over to connect to the dream. Help and resources will come to you as you share what is in you, together with the helping hands of many the dream will come to pass!

As you are reading this book, I will be sharing my dream with you as well and you will feel a connection with me for life, because our dreams are aligning with each other. Read this book repeatedly as needed to keep it close when enduring hardships, keep yourself sharp and always keep moving forward in faith. I will share my dream with you and I want you to be vulnerable to share your dream with me and others. I want to assure you that failure is not an option the only way you fail is to quit! Good success is yours for the taking, when you speak passionately of your dream, it allows emotions and joy to be released, which others will pick up on. Share your dream of hope and aspiration, and others will come and support your dream! Let everyone know, how bad you want it, Dr. King's life was fueled by the dream. Your dream is what gives you strength and vigor to tenaciously change your world.

Your dream is an inner assignment that transforms the outer environment. Let me say that again, your dream is an inner assignment that transforms the outer environment. Your dreaming is critical for you to reach your place of destiny. Dr. Martin Luther King had a dream of freedom and equality, living your dream will liberate you from restrictions, which come to encroach you from doing great things. In your dream, there is a freedom and a liberty that sets the captives free. Life as you know it is captive, limited, and restricted but your dream will promote you to prominence. Whatever is holding you back, whatever was holding you down, whatever impediment is blocking you dream, break the limits of your life. Living the dream, will be like living as a king. You are the super hero in your dream and nothing can stop you. In the dream, nothing can hinder you from living the life you were ordained to live. Dr. King had a dream that one day, everyone in America could be free to be whatever they wanted to be. Dr. King endured much hardship and persecution to birth his dream.

You and I must also understand that with a dream comes anti-dreamers, antagonist, pessimistic and unbelievers that we must all live above. Don't go down to their ignorant level, stay on the dream wall and repair all the breaches in your life. Nehemiah understood this when he stated in Nehemiah 6:3 "I am carrying on a great project and cannot go down. Why should the work stop while I leave it and go down to you?" We must learn to live above the distractions to be able to see our dreams complete. This devastating vision of Nehemiah homeland and the wall that was there protection was a picture of their relationship with God. Nehemiah was heart broken to see the wall of protect and his homeland tore down. Nehemiah went to work to rebuild the wall of protection. What has to be rebuilt in your life to bring protection, healing and restoration? Nehemiah went to work on the wall. The enemy's tried to stop the work. Know that when you are trying to do somethings great enemies will come out of the wood work! Hater will manifest who you don't even know, to fight against the vision. Nehemiah 4-Sanballat and Tobiah and Geshem were three enemies of the Jewish people. They were set out to stop the vision of Nehemiah, and suppress the people of God. Nehemiah's wall construction plan was set in motion. Nehemiah put all the workers and the guards in place and the work begun. Nehemiah was focused on His assignment. He didn't let the distractions distract from doing the work God called Him to do. With the help of God, the vision of rebuilding the wall was complete in a miraculous amount of time. The wall was completed in 52 days. What should take years can be completed in days. Let got to work on your vision, how bad do you want it?

What is your Dream? Say it! What is your Dream? Say it again! What is your Dream? Say it louder! What is your Dream? Say it like you mean it! Everyone's dream is different! Don't get caught up trying to live someone else's dream and competing with others. Don't get caught up asking other people about what they think about the dream God gave you. Dreams are tailor made to suit you only. Dreams are defined, dreams are custom and personalized.

Chapter 4

WRITE THE VISSION!

I want to segue by saying Psalms 46:1- "God is our refuge and strength, an ever-present help in trouble." The dream or vision of what you see is for your eyes only and we must see the dream first through the eyes of faith! Once again, write it down, what you see in the dream and all the pieces will soon fall into place. I want to encourage you from the Bible Habakkuk 2:2-3 says, "Write down the revelation and make it plain on tablets so that a herald may run with it. For the revelation awaits on appointed time; it speaks of the end and will not prove false." As you write down the dream, goal or vision, clarity comes. Write down your dreams because I believe it will be a road map to your place of destiny! For the vision is yet for the appointed time, and it hasteth toward the end, and shall not lie: though it tarries, wait for it; because it will surely come, it will not delay. Our meeting in the pages of this book is an appointed time for both of us to do what hasn't been done before. You have some goals and dreams to accomplish! After all, you reading this book is one of my dreams come true!

Dreams can happen for you we are being freed together my friend. We are liberating ourselves into a small sect of society that was bold enough to go for the dream. Liberation is coming to you, setting yourself apart as one that wanted the dream bad enough. Say it until you believe it! The first person you need to win is yourself! No one will help you and no one will believe in you if they don't see the fire of desire in your eyes! Romans 10:17 "consequently, faith comes from hearing the message, and the message is heard through the word about Christ." Read your dream daily and revisit the vision as often as you can! Read it out loud, faith comes by hearing so reinforce your dream by speaking it. The dream is the goal and faith is the exercise that creates dream realities. You have to convince yourself to believe that "with God all things are possible" Mark 10:27.

Your dream is possible and you can do it! Join the club of living the incredible dream life! You must fight the forces of evil in order to achieve the dream! Your dreams and goals will happen but it comes with a price. Most people are not willing to pay the cost of success and not everybody is willing to pay the price to live the dream just don't give up! Some people don't have a dream or a vision and die off in the wilderness wandering around going nowhere fast. Just complaining and blaming others for their unwillingness to fight the good fight of faith!

Numbers 14:33 "your children will be shepherds here for forty years, suffering for your unfaithfulness, until the last of your bodies lies in the wilderness." Leading the right path to invest quality time, in un-dream-like activity is like building a golden calf instead of building a sure house! Matthew 7:25 "The rain came down, the streams rose, and the winds blew and beat against that house; yet it did not fall, because it had its foundation on the rock."

The rains are adversities of life and floods are personal attacks. Winds are distractions that entice us daily not to focus on the dream. You will not fail, and your faith will make you whole. Your foundation is sure and it will stand the test of time. God is the foundation of your life! God has our back and has a dream for each one of us to fulfill! God had a dream or a vision for his people, and they copped out! They settled and died rather than live and thrive in their promised land. Numbers 13:31 "But the men who had gone up with him said, "we can't attack those people; they are stronger than we are." Have you talked yourself into settling? What is your excuse for not entering your promised land that is a fruitful, pregnant place? The promised land is flowing with milk and honey! The promised land was the place God was taking his people to and was a gift given by God; it was an inheritance, but whether we get it or not, is all up to you. The promise of God is in him Yes, and in him Amen, to the glory of God through us 2 Corinthians 1:20.

How bad do you want it? How bad do you want what God has for you? Dream Chaser–You have to be a dream chaser! Why not add your name to the list of dream chasers? I won't say my dream was as universally emancipating as Dr. King's dream, but the dream gave me the same liberating power to lift a life from what it was into the dream to be. A dream will give you courage to believe when others doubt! A dream will give you the power to live and to see your full potential, and will change the course of your life. As you are reading this book, I want you to expect change, a new realm of courage to overtake you! Deuteronomy 31:6-8 Moses calls for Joshua, and tells him that it is his turn to take over, and Moses speaks four things to him.

1. Be Strong

2. Have good courage
3. Fear not
4. Don't be afraid.

Be strong and of a good courage, fear not, nor be afraid of them: for the LORD thy God, he it is that doth go with thee; he will not fail thee, nor forsake thee. Then Moses called unto Joshua, and said unto him in the sight of all Israel, be strong and of a good courage: for thou must go with this people and lead them into the promise land which the LORD HATH sworn unto their fathers to give them; and thou shalt cause them to inherit it. Did you receive this word, God is with you now, forget about the past, and focus on the future. He is with us, God will not fail us, God is our refuge and strength, A very present help in trouble. I want you to be on the watch for breakthroughs and get excited because your dream and vision still lives. Restoration and resurrection is coming to your life. The dream is leaping inside your soul and is alive and kicking, do what you need to get up and pursue the dream.

Chapter 5

NO EXCUSES!

I want to encourage you about a great woman that wanted it bad enough and made no excuses for the challenges that stood tall before her. She pulled it down and conquered the mountain in front of her. Her name is Helen Keller! Helen Keller was the first deaf and blind person to earn a Bachelor of Arts Degree. What is your problem? Your problems will not be able to stand against your dream. Helen Keller is a picture of determination as she overcame her obstacles and became famous. Helen Keller became a great American Author and Political Activist and Lecturer!

2 Corinthians 10:4-5 "The weapons we fight with are not the weapons of the world. On the contrary, they have divine power to demolish strongholds. We demolish arguments and every pretension that sets itself up against the knowledge of God, and we take captive every thought to make it obedient to Christ." This means we have to delete, erase, forget every negative thought that come, into our minds. Know this, in life we will all encounter challenges. But how do you handle the challenges that come your way? How you face your challenges will determine the quality of your life. Challenges are part of

the growth process and come to see if we have mastered this level for success to come! Challenges are part of the faith process and knowing that deep down on the inside of you lies the answer to your current problems. Challenges push us to seek deeper past the flesh to bring physical and spiritual change into our lives. The missing links in the chain will appear to solve our problems. All it takes is getting in agreement with the mindset of God almighty, "I can do all things through Christ strengthening me"–Philippians 4:13.

Your willingness to face the problems with an "I can do" attitude will make the difference. Solving the problems in life will reward you greatly! We must face the giants in our life to live the dream. The story of David is a great story as David was the youngest in his family, and he started as a shepherd boy with a few sheep. Yet David lived to become King of Israel and Judah. David had faith to face his foes and a confidence that with God all things were possible for him. David had an "I can do" mindset. While Saul was king, the kingdom of Israel was under attack by the Philistine's. The great champion fighter was threating the people of God and David's older brothers were in the army of Saul. One day his father sent him to the battle to deliver a goody box filled with cheese and crackers. When he reached the Battle there is no one fighting, and all David heard was the enemies Champ Goliath bragging and boasting about how victorious he was! Goliath said, send your best and nobody moved. You must be willing to move when others are paralyzed by fears, and doubts. Nobody was willing to fight! You must be willing to fight the giants in your life. Giants are what stands before you and your dream. Nobody is willing to fight for the Kingdom of God! At the time, David was about the age of seventeen, and full of great potential and talent. We just need the right situation to bring out the greatest in us and release our potential.

As David heard the defiance of Goliath, courage arose up in him and he went to King Saul and said, "I'll fight him." Understand this, you have to fight for what you want in life! If it is to be, it is up to me! Fight for your right to live a privileged life. David's brothers knew David was ambitious and that is the spirit that makes dreams come true. They tried to deter David from his dream. Saul tried to put his armor on David, but David was already covered.

1 Samuel 17:34-37 David said, to Saul, "Your servant was tending his father's sheep. When a lion or a bear came and took a lamb from the flock, I went out after him and attacked him, and rescued *it* from his mouth; and when he rose up against me, I seized him by his beard and struck him and killed him. "Your servant has killed both the lion and the bear; and this uncircumcised Philistine will be like one of them, since he has taunted the armies of the living God." And David said, The Lord who delivered me from the paw of the lion and from the paw of the bear, He will deliver me from the hand of this Philistine." And Saul said to David, "Go, and may the Lord be with you." 1 Samuel 17:48 "As the Philistine moved closer to attack him, David ran quickly toward the battle line to meet him." Procrastination is giving place for the devil, don't allow the devil to steal your faith. David ran quickly to the battle, and put his hand into his bag and took from it a stone and slung it, the stone struck the Philistine on his forehead and sank into his forehead, so that he fell on his face to the ground. Thus David prevailed over the Philistine with a sling and a stone. 1 Samuel 17:51 "David ran and stood over him. He took hold of the Philistines sword and drew it from the sheath. After he killed

him, he cut off his head with the sword. When the Philistines saw that their hero was dead, they turned and ran."

David fought for his dream and vision to come to pass. What you don't confront you never conquer. David faced his enemy and was rewarded for his actions. You too must fight to see your future blessed to be a blessing. David's whole life changed with one fight! Understand what I just told you, one fight can change your life. Great riches were given to David, and he became part of the royal family and didn't have any more taxes to pay. I want you to get ready to fight the good fight of faith one more time, this time it will be different. How you handle problems, will end with different outcomes as different situations arise causing a life altering series of events that will yield you a new life!

Let's work on taping into the rich destinies awaiting us as we pursue our dreams! Greater is waiting for you like oil in the ground, waiting for someone bold enough to keep drilling, keep hoping and keep believing until the riches of living your dream shoots up in your life. Just tap into your dream, and riches and new destinies will be conquered in your life! Are you still a dreamer? A dreamer we should all know about, is Joseph. Joseph was about the age of seventeen when he dreamed of himself being great. How do you see yourself? Dreams help shape your self-identity. Genesis 37:5 "Joseph had a dream, and when he told it to his brothers, they hated him all the more." Joseph's dream in the beginning made life hard for him. I want to let you know things will get hard, things will get worse before things get better, but in the end, you will say it was all worth it. But how bad do you want it!

Most people are not dreamers anymore. They've allowed the world, society, people and their past to steal their dreams! Joseph was hated by the support of family. The family was to be the covering. The family is to be the protectors of the dream. Joseph was hated by siblings that were to help the dream become a reality! The family is to be a safe-haven where dreams can be released, cultivated, crafted and perfected! A dream and a dreamer is to be loved and embraced, not hated! You must pose a new confidence in your dream. A dreamer must be ready to endure a few hardships as a good soldier to see their dream become a true reality (2 Timothy 2:3).

Be loved and embraced, not hated or sold out. Not hated and sold out. Joseph held on to His dream to be a blessing to the world and to save His family. Joseph wanted His dream bad enough to be a slave. Thrown into prison and yet became one the greatest men of His time.

Chapter 6

DREAM CHASER!

Dr. King was a dream chaser! You too are a dream chaser, let's settle that argument in your head. Do not stay in denial any longer, embrace the dream. Dr. King kept pursuing his dream, people that were trying to kill him couldn't stop the dream chaser. The bombing and threats couldn't stop him from chasing the dream. Become a dream chaser today!

Are you chasing your dream? I can remember watching our home teams, the New York Giants and the New York Jets play at the Meadowlands. They said that New York couldn't fit in New Jersey! Well I beg to differ, both of our Pro Football Teams were housed in New Jersey. As I watched I can remember, dreaming of myself playing on that same field one day. I can remember dreaming of myself playing in the Meadowland Stadium in East Rutherford New Jersey. The fat, round, dumpy, little boy from a small little city, like Passaic New Jersey, population of 45,000 in 1965 had a dream to play Professional Football. Passaic in its small beginnings produced some good football fruit, one person that was a Passaic product was Jack Tatum. Jack graduated from Passaic High School and was nicknamed the Assassin! You can't get a better name than that. Jack was Passaic's claim to fame and played nine years in the NFL. Jack Tatum was a Pro- Bowler and a Super Bowl Champion with the Raiders. I can remember meeting Jack one day, in the housing projects of Passaic, wow that was a day to remember. Know now, that the people you meet take part of you fulfilling your dream. As a young boy meeting Jack Tatum, exposed me to what I could be, because of his greatness and distinction. Some people exist and others persist and conquer life.

The distinction that will define you is that you never settled, never give up and never stop believing in your dream or yourself. In the City of Passaic, New Jersey very few have made it to the NFL, and I am honored to be listed with the great men that did make it. I'm sure they too have dedicated great efforts to making their dreams come true.

I couldn't run fast, I wasn't athletic but I had a dream and I dreamed of getting my dream job. Playing in the NFL with an elite group of men of about 2000 chosen tough players to be on the roaster! Don't limit yourself, dreams are free, it won't cost you anything,

Tyronne Stowe and little brother Durelle, with his Pittsburgh Steeler Jersey is it a coincidence or faith?

but if you don't live your dream, you will regret, sitting idle for life. Your dream is free to your own imagination. Let the dream take you to a life that money can't buy. When you start dreaming, money isn't usually a resource you need. It does not cost you anything to dream, but if you don't dream it will cost you a bankrupt life. Start dreaming and every resource you need to make the dream happen will be deposited in your life! My dream job was to be an NFL player and I made it!

Don't back up off your confession. Hebrews 10:23-24 "Let us hold unswervingly to the hope we profess, for he who promised is faithful. And let us consider how we may spur one another on toward love and good deeds." No wavering, stand firm in you dream confession my friend.

First you must convince yourself, what you want to be, when you grow up. How old are you now? Have you grown up yet? Do you know what you want to be? If you don't know what you want, you will fall for anything. When you have a target, you must aim to hit the mark. It is 100% definite that you will never hit any target you are not aiming for. The dream is a mark in your life and a goal or target one desires to hit! Most of us, have not targeted our lives which is why we are living unfulfilled lives. We must press toward the mark, that God has for us to reach. We must aim now for the dream bull's eye! I believe that every little boy, has the same type of dream at one time or another doing something great! For some odd reason, I can't tell you to this day, why I thought I could make it!

Baseball and Basketball are great sports, but there is something about Football, ruff housing, running around and crashing into each other, that caught my heart. Boys can't walk down the hall at school without hitting, throwing, running or jumping over each other! Boys are built to love the idea of being the tuff guy, or being a big boy! Ok maybe that is just for me, but football is the # 1 Boy's Sport in America!

At the time of my dream, I was unconfident, overweight, shy, nervous, round, piggy, short, 11 or 12-year-old little boy. I know some of my old teammates would say, that Stowe hasn't changed a bit! What I want you to know is that dreaming is healthy, not problematic and gives vision and direction to one's life. Proverbs 29:18 "Where there is no revelation, people cast off restraint; but blessed is the one who heeds wisdom's instruction." A dream gives you a vision of what you will be and what you're called to do. A dream gives vision to where you are going and once you know where you are going, it's easier to get there. The dream is vision, keeping you on track, with healthy habits, with productive paths, drawing you closer to dream attainment. Dreams and visions keep us focused so declare that you will pursue your dream. Dreams and visions help you keep your eye on the prize! How bad do you want the dream prize? Dr. King started boycotting things that were not right in his life! Sometimes in life you got to learn, to sit it out and that things are not for you. We have to acquire the discipline, to boycott. We have to be willing to sit some things out! We need to learn to let some things pass and let the world know, "I'm not taking it anymore!" Knowing what your dream is, will help you segregate yourself from un-dream like activity. Boycotting was a decision made to make the dream work!

Boycotting caused crystallization of the dream and was a way to adopt new ideas to make the dream come to pass. Boycotting any dysfunctional or unrighteous acts that would hinder the dream. We must employ every plausible option to draw the dream into reality. What are you living with that you know is not right? What are you tolerating in your life that is not part of the dream? What is holding you back? It's time to boycott and sit out of any activity that would dilute dream productivity! Sit it out! The neighborhood boys were starting up a football game at the school across the street from my house, on Summer Street in Passaic, New Jersey and I wanted to play very bad but never played with them before. I didn't know that the two best people couldn't be on the same sides. The two best people were the captains and they picked until the teams were filled and after waiting, guess what? I didn't get picked. I had to sit it out! I was boycotted from playing the game, involuntarily! I felt very bad and felt I had a right to play, but they were prejudiced against me. Yes, prejudice towards me because they didn't know how good I was and they prejudged me! I went home very upset but with a mindset that, this would never happen to me again. It was all just a matter of, how bad do you want it? How bad do you want to play?

What do you do when people tell you can't play? What do you do when you don't get picked? What do you do when things don't go your way? How do you handle rejection? How do you handle set-backs? This is what created this mantra in my life. How bad do you want it? As an 11-year-old boy I was faced with answering this question, how bad do you want it? From that day forward until now, these six words have challenged and pushed me on a wonderful journey. These six words, will lift you to great heights in life and fuel you to believe in your dream!

When you have victory and success you will see these six words undergirding your life. When you are down and defeated these six words not let you stay there as you will cause you to rise to the occasion. You will become more than a conqueror in your life. Joshua 1:5 "No one will be able to stand against you all the days of your life. As

I was wish Moses, so I will be with you; I will never leave you nor forsake you." There shall not any man be able to stand before thee all the days of thy life! Little did I know that these six words, would take me around the world. Not getting picked, that day has fueled my life to do incredible things as I set out to show the boy's I got it too!

It's nothing wrong with you validating yourself! John 15:16 "You did not choose me, I chose you and appointed you." God appointed you to have a fruitful life! How bad do you want it? One of the greatest talents I have seen come up was Allen Iverson. I watched him at George Town, wow what a great talent! He was the first round pick for the Philadelphia 76'ers! I like the 76'ers, because Dr. J, Daryl Dawkins, Maurice Cheeks Vinny the microwave, but Allen Iverson single handedly took them to the playoffs. The Sky was the limit for this man talent. I'm not sure if Allen really asked himself, the six words! How bad do you want it?

One of the times we all remember is him berating a coach who wanted him to practice! He didn't believe in practice and his talent only caused him to fall short. He was a great player and is a player to be remembered but what could he have been if he practiced, and perfection was his priority! Whatever opportunities and chances we have left in life let's give it our all! I want you to push past your past! See where you are today and start preparing for your future! God has great things in your future! 1 Corinthians 2:9–10 "What no eye has seen, what no ear has heard, and what no human mind has conceived the things God has prepared for those who love him. These are the things God has revealed to us by his spirit. The spirit searches all things even the deep things of God."

Dreams live in the realm of the spirit and the spirit is unseen realm of possibilities. You must learn to dream and see yourself differently. You must determine how bad you really want it. All my peers, ex-teammates and coaches knew that I was not the most talented, most athletic, the biggest, strongest, fastest or smartest, but one thing I knew, that everybody else didn't is that, I was going to live my dream! Most people don't want it bad enough, do you? Most people will not pay the price for success. Most people will not allow themselves to endure and develop into the great person you were created to be! Problems create pressure, under pressure diamonds manifest! Can you let the pressure of today force you to being a diamond in the ruff? Who you are now is not the person you will be. Things will get better, don't stay stuck, and keep working on yourself. Most people will not do the things to succeed. It all boils down to how bad do you want it?

Chapter 7
SMALL BEGINNINGS!

Zechariah 4:10 "Who dares despise the day of small things." The Civil Rights movement started because one lady refused to give up her seat on the bus. Her name is Rosa Parks, her life speaks to all of us all knowing that God has prepared a seat for us and we must not abdicate our seat in Gods master plan. This little act caused spiritual reform in America. This woman's little stance caused an avalanche of inequity to be brought down. She faced the challenge to bring equal opportunities for all people! Today you have the right and opportunity to change your life. No matter how bad it is, get started today forming a frame work for the future. The dream is nothing tangible in the beginning. But don't despise it. The dream is a seed, a thought, a premonition planted in the ground of your hearts. The dream starts out small and grows and takes over your life naturally! I want you to sit back and watch the small beginning of a dream seed take you from glory to glory and from faith to faith! This dream seed will grow in your life and bare much fruit for you! It will start small and snowball into an unstoppable storm of blessings, let's get it started!

Time is the most important resource we have on Earth and we have wasted a lot of it in riotous, unproductive and suppressed living. As you are reading this book, you are mentally positioning yourself to get things in order to start the dream. My dear neighborhood friend Clark Linsey lived up the street from me on Summer Street in Passaic New Jersey, and was the one who turned me on to organized Football. I became part of the 2nd Ward Association. What organizations do you have to join to make the dream happen? What club must you be a part of to bring out the dream in you? What needed skills must you acquire to live the dream? For some of you, it may be joining the right Church, for others, it may be to join a counseling session or joining a gym or returning back to school to land the dream job! Whatever it is, let get it started today! Time is of the essence and time is running out. I joined the 2nd Warders Association Little League Team and my life has never been the same. Right where you are today in life, let's get started on the dream that awaits.

Our head coach of our team was Carl Marsano. Coach Carl was a big old school Italian man and we called him Coach Carl. Coach Carl was the first coach I ever had. The sooner you get a coach in your life, the sooner the dream can be a reality! Lay down your ego, and know that God has placed people in your life to help you bring the dream to reality! In every area of your life you need a coach to teach you how to bring the dream in! If you ever plan to be great you need a coach. If you want to improve, get a coach, a mentor, a father, a friend. You need O.P.E! Other People's Experience- this will accelerate your life. Coach Carl was a great coach and a great man. Coach Carl had a great family and they opened up their house for us and made a gym in his garage. His wonderful wife would make us great spaghetti dinners with those big meat balls. Coach Carl said, "Stowe you're great" and would tell me that I had what it takes to make it Big! Coach Carl saw something in me that I couldn't see. Surround yourself as early as possible with positive people that speak good tidings into your life. Coach Carl planted words in my life that touched my heart that I am still gleaming from today!

Coach Carl watered us often with words of affirmation. We would watch movies and films at his house. Coach Carl watered us with much time and as a result we blossomed with confidence. As

THE PASSAIC CITIZEN   Thursday, February 24, 1983

TYRONE STOWE, member of the Passaic High School's football team, is presented with the Athletic Scholastic Award by the 2nd Ward Association at its Sports Award Dinner. With Stowe are (left) Carl Marzano, coach of the Junior League, and Vinny Magliarditi, operator of the luncheonette at Main and Monroe in Passaic.

***Coach Carl Marzano and Vinny Magliarditi presents
award to Tyronne Stowe***

little boy's, Coach Carl told me that I could go a long way all we had to do was trust him and listen to what he said. Proverbs 24:7-For by wise guidance you will wage war, and in abundance of counselors there is victory. Victory come when you have guidance and wise counsel in your life.

"Gracious words are as a honeycomb sweet to the soul, and health to the bones." Proverbs 16:24 A healthy and fruitful life is having people in place to speak what you seek. Coach Carl was that person for me, he gave me the confidence that I needed. At my home there was some dysfunction and abuse. I wouldn't say that I suffered tragically but disciplining children should be done with skill and purpose, and never done out of anger. Most people are living with chips on their shoulders. They have never got free of the old hurts and pains of the past. Most people take out their frustrations on the closest people around them! You have to get free from the past to let the new life of dreams come! In life, you will find hurt people, hurt other people. They cast the weight of pain on everybody in their path! We must see our young people as precious gifts, tender and pliable for success development! As Adults, we must be equipped and understanding of the potential greatness that lies within all of us. As parents, we must never adopt any behavior that doesn't enhance, encourage or assure a child's mental stability. Verbal abuse and name calling can cut deeper than a knife, because what happens is the dream picture is being distorted. The dream is taking on a negative, notion. Scared children don't handle life correctly, scared children second guess themselves, worry and are more apt to sickness and nervous breakdowns. But a healthy childhood breeds confidence. Our households should be a safe haven of love. But far too often we find ourselves in a pit of discouragement. Joseph kept His faith that God would bring His dream to past. Genesis 37:9 Then he had another dream, and he told it to his brothers. "Listen," he said, "I had another dream, and this time the sun and moon and eleven stars were bowing down to me." And he told it to his father, and to his brethren; and his father rebuked him, and said unto him, what is this dream that thou hast dreamed? Shall I and thy mother and thy brethren indeed come to bow down ourselves to thee to the earth? Joseph spoke his dream again but this time in the presence of his father. Surely Joseph's father knows that his own seed is to be fruitful and greater than that of the father! A true father expects nothing less than each generation growing greater, and passing on wealth!

Dreaming of playing football and for a better life became my escape. Things at home weren't bad, but it wasn't a dream center for support and encouragement. It wasn't a safe haven for dream reinforcement. Can you understand, that when you dare to do something great, life changing, doing something no one has ever done before in your family, your family might not know what you need. Let me tell you, you may not get all the support and backing from your family. And it's not that they are against you or that they don't love you. They just can't see how special you are in the dream. They just can't see how fragile the Dream is in you. The dream comes in a package, you are the package, the label is marked handled with care. Life can take you and toss you around and you feel like nothing! You don't feel special, but Satan is a liar. You are a special delivery a special package full of dreams! The truth of the matter is they can't see the dream in you yet. And in the heat of life's battles, name calling, degrading, cursing, and beatings sometimes take place instead of dream protection. To live your dream, find someone you can trust. Find a coach, a family member, or a friend that will speak encouraging words into your life to help you take off the limits in your life. Keep positive people in your corner, it will thrust your dream forward. Find someone genuine you can listen and learn from like Coach Carl who invested in me. Dreams are realized by assembling a dream team. No one can make it by themselves, surround yourself with motivating people. Surround yourself with people that have common goals and ambitions. Live the dream you want; be a lawyer, doctor, movie star, or to play Pro-Football! It's up to you it's time to get started!

To play little league, you had to weigh, 115 or so, I truly don't recall exactly what my weight was, but I knew I was 20 pounds or more over weight to play. Are you over weight? Are you carrying excess baggage? Is life pounding up on you? Is the weight of worry piling up and getting you down? How bad you want to lay aside the weight or the sin that so easily beset us? What sins do you need to lay aside that is working against you? Gluttony is a sin! Whenever we over indulge in unproductive anti dream behavior and habits, we break down the frame work of dream success. Is your daily activity lining up with your dream? I know I'm not the only one that had the challenge of being overweight to play little league! What are you doing to overcome, your heavy issues in life? I was told by some to get ready for next year, there's not enough time for you to make weight. Why are we allowing other's assessments to dictate our future? Why do we accept what's said and not being dream led?

You have the power to make life into what you want it to be. Why do we except less than the best? At that time, my Coach stepped in, took me off the scale and said, "Stowe, do you want to play?" I said "yes, I do!" Coach bent down looked me in the eye, and said, "how bad do you want it?" "How bad do you want to play?" I don't remember my answer, but the next thing I remembered Coach saying, "you got to do what I tell you to do, and you can play!" I had a goal, I had a dream. I had a vision to play pro football. Coach Carl put me on a diet and I worked out twice a day, with weights and running. Coach Carl even took me, to a Turkish bath! It was a steam shower place to help you lose weight and it was hot and it worked. With Coach Carl's guidance, I made the weight and I had a good little league career. We made it to the championship, but we lost. I was MVP of our team! MVP!

In your life, you have to change how you see yourself. You must possess a MVP attitude. The world's most valuable person! The world is the stage and people are extras and co-stars on your show. See yourself as an up and coming star! Start seeing yourself as a super star in the making. See yourself as an Academy Award Winner. You are the movie star in your life. You are the Most Valuable Person in your reality sitcom of life. And it's all about you, making the dreams happen. People are watching, how you handle life and waiting to see how you ride the wave of life's ups and downs. Seeing how you are led in life and land securely in your dream. The audience of friends and family and followers are learning from you how to win in life. Fans from near and far lives will be changed and strengthened and encouraged by seeing you stay in character, to live the dream. You are an example to many people you know and many people you don't know. Just keep walking in the image of the dream as you have for yourself. People are watching to see how you handle life and limitations and dealing with problems.

I want to get you stirred up, you can do this! Walk through every hurdle life dictates and make your name Great. Your home town, your birthplace, your city, your state, will never forget you leaving your mark. The accomplishments you make will set you apart from society.

42

You are the star of your show, in the end you will ride off into the sun set of your dream!

At Passaic High School, we were coached by a man named Tom Elsasser, who challenged us mentally and filled a need in our community. He was a white man, in a mixed neighborhood, Blacks, Whites, Spanish, Mexican, Dominican, Indians, Poland's, calling us Son's. But the game kept changing, whoever he was with, at the time was the #1 son!

Tyronne Stowe with friends and teammates Craig Heywood, Marshal Grier, Kevin Bryant, Nate Heywood and Anthony Kenner

He gave us all attention; and made us feel special, like we were the only ones that mattered. We all voluntarily competed for his affection, to be called the #1 son! Under Coach Tom Elsasser's, we won two state championships. On our teams, God assembled a great cast of athletes; I was not the best, the fastest or the strongest. One of my high school team mates was Craig Iron Head Heywood. Tyronne

Stowe with friend Craig Iron Head Heywood at sport center down town Passaic, New Jersey and we won two state Championships together. Could you imagine playing in his shadow? He was a 1st round draft pick of the New Orleans Saints in 1988. Craig was a great player, and got a scholarship to the University of Pittsburgh, the Pittsburg Panthers, and made history, I believe the only other person to be so good, from High School was his older brother Nate who went to Pittsburgh University on a scholarship two for one! The university wanted Craig that bad! Craig's older brother Nate the skate, was a good player too. But he wouldn't have received a scholarship alone from Pittsburgh. Nate was much smaller than his little brother Craig Iron head Heywood, but Nate was pound for pound the hardest hitter I've seen! Craig Heywood went on to the NFL and played for 11 years, with the New Orleans Saints, Chicago Bears, Atlanta Falcons and St Louis Rams. Craig earned an All Pro team appearance also.

***Tyrone with friend Craig "Iron Head" Haywooed
at sports center downtown Passiac NJ***

We really never got to see the full potential of Craig Iron Head Heywood. Craig was my friend from the age of ten and we met at the Boys Club Downtown, what an intimidating sight was seeing a 9-year-old that look like a midget man, he shocked me, as I thought I was tuff, but this little man from the hood was a sight to see!! And his little brother Nate was equally menacing and deviant. Those were the good old days since then our neighborhood super star Craig Iron Head Heywood has passed away, but he has four boy's carrying his athletic torch. One of Craig's sons, followed in his father's footsteps.

Cameron Heywood, who was drafted in the 2011 NFL draft. Cameron Heywood was the first round pick of the Pittsburgh Steelers. Cameron grew up in Pittsburgh and was going back home to put on the Black and Gold. I just want to say, on behalf of your dad, that he is very, very proud of you, and so am I. Charlotte, you have done a great job as a mother, keep up the great work in living the dream!

In high school, playing in the shadow of Craig Iron head Heywood was tough. Coach Elsasser, nicknamed me "Slow train Stowe." Tyronne Slow Train Stowe, doesn't sound to promising, I ran a 5.8 forty-yard dash, can I even call that a dash? One thing I did was work hard. I often worked with my dad during the summers, and sometimes on the weekends. My dad was a hard worker. I saw how hard he worked, and I knew that hard work was the key for success. Seeing my father, drive a truck by day, foreman at a plastic company by night, and bar tender on weekend's to support, his wife and five kids gave me a work ethic and a determination to make something good out of my life. My goal was to make my parents proud of me. Showing them, by working hard, that I too was a true Hustler! A Hustler, was a person that would do what it takes to make it happen. A hustler is a person, not too proud to get their hands dirty! A hustler doesn't have everything, skills or education, but works very feverishly to accomplish the goal. A hustler, was one that lacked resources or finances, but by hustling, and working hard they get it done! Are you getting it done? Are You a Hustler? As I watched my dad, hustle driving trucks, I knew loading and unloading trucks wasn't for me! I wasn't cut out to do that type of manual labor. I had to find something different to do!

Football was my dream and Coach Tom would tell us we were full of potential. How bad do you want it? He would scream it loud for everybody to hear, and at difficult times I can still hear him screaming "you don't want it bad enough!" I want, the title of this book to echo and be imprinted on your mind forever, like it has for me the past 34 years! How bad do you want it? I pray that by the end of this book, you will exhibit the courage tenacity of character to be certain that you want it bad enough! I want to coach you into your dream. I want it for you badly! Coach Elsasser would scream as loud as he could "you don't want it bad enough?" "You're cuffin it! You're cuffin it!" What does cuffing it mean? When you get cuffs, they cut the pants to fit the person's height and the roll the material up to make the cuff! Then they stitch the material for a permanent length. Have you cuffed it? God didn't design you to wear a cuff. God wants us all to live long, no cutting away of the dream! Could it be that you were meant to live long and without restrictions and limitations but you settled for cuffing it? What should have been the dream we cut short. What should have been the dream is now rolled up into a cuff. What should have been the dream is made shorter, limited dreams now stitched up permanently altered never to be let down again. Have you let life cause you to cuff your destiny that wasn't your dream? Don't cuff it, get back to work! Peter spoke very boldly in saying, "But Peter declared, "Even if I have to die with you, I will never disown you." And all the other disciples said the same." Matthew 26:35 and in Matthew 26:75 "Then Peter remembered the word Jesus had spoken: "Before the rooster crows, you will disown me three times." And he went outside and wept bitterly." Peter cuffed it and went back to fishing. Peter was supposed to let his faith hang out, but he denied our lord and savior three times and he cuffed it and went back to the flesh! Peter did however, get back to work and was a fisher of men and preached, Pentecostal message and birthed the Church and 3000 souls came to know the Lord! It's time for us to get back to work. Don't cuff it! Let the dream hang. Redeem the time for the day are evil!

Chapter 8

DREAM PREGNANCY!

Through my dad, Coach Carl, and Coach Elsasser, that hard work produced dream pregnancy! The dreams are to be conceived, carried and delivered. The umbilical cord feeds and nourishes your dream. Hard work pushes you through the developmental fetal stages before you can actually see your dream come into reality. During this period change is taking place. Your looks are changing, body is changing, mind is changing, image is changing and eating habits are changing. Your size is changing as you get bigger in order to support the dream. Hard work is feeding the dream. The dream is your baby, and is the most important thing in the world to you. The dream is the one thing you know has been entrusted unto you from God! Dream pregnancy means the dream is already living inside of you, and conception of the dream has already taken place: Conception is the act of receiving a notion or idea and when potential and desire kiss and produced a love child called a dream.

The life of the dream is seeing yourself in an exalted state somewhere in the near future. Conception is your dream living inside of you maturing and growing in you. Do not abort your dream, say yes to your dream, today. The seed of thoughts, has penetrated the womb and the dream is given life to you! No one can visualize the dream conception at first, however the miracle has already taken place within. You may not be showing any sign of the dream pregnancy yet, but let me announce that you are pregnant. You are now carrying the dream. Along the way you will feel like giving up, taking the path of least resistance but I want to assist you in delivery. Do not allow anything to cause you to terminate the dream. Push your way through and deliver the dream in your life. Keep your mind focused on how beautiful life will be living the dream! Dream development and hard work is what feeds the dream and is what causes the dream to grow. Conception has already taken place, hard work is the pre-natal care to develop and grow shape the dream into existence!

I worked hard in the weight room, study hall and class room. They told us hard work pays big dividends (that's what they told me) Coach Elsasser challenged us to put our time in to see the rewards. He said, "hard work makes the dreams happen!" What hardship are you dealing with? Hard work is the key. Stop avoiding what is not right in your life. Deal with the hard problems in your life, Deal with the problem with it will produce your baby! What hardship are you encountering? Is it sickness, divorce, bankruptcy, unemployment or whatever it may be? Take one day at a time and do what you can today. Break it down into small pieces. Work every day feverishly toward personal improvement and face the challenges that lay ahead of you with hard work. The challenges of the day will be testimonies of tomorrow and your dream will not fail you! Hard work is the labor pains that will birth the dream. How bad do you want it? Want it bad enough! Hard work pays off!

Coach Elsasser and hard work brought out my potential. I got into better shape and worked to improve myself. I cut some time off my 40-yard dash times and I was able to improve my mental and physical condition. The battle is won between the ears. Your mind, is a terrible thing to waste! Your mind conceived the dream and your mind starts the dream. The mind is where the dream expansion takes place. Dreams make a difference in your life! How you think and how you see yourself is critical to dream success! I kept thinking about the dream and it gave me insight, on what I had to do to make the dream happen! This is called meditation! We have all meditated in the past about something. Meditation is continued or extended transcendental thoughts, reflections and contemplations. We typically use this powerful tool of meditation adversely to our own peril. We sit back and invest quality time thinking on negative possibilities. We think and envision those bad things happening, problems and situations but by worrying and rehearsing these things we ignorantly have created our own reality. Think of what you want and not on how things are! Please take some time now to purposely meditate on your dream!

I suggest that you begin to incorporate daily meditation as your normal routine in your life! I kept meditating on the dream day and night. I kept seeing myself in the future; successful, accomplished, and empowered by the inner dream appearing. Dream meditation caused us to do what is needed to be done. Make a list of what needs to be done for you to live the dream. By you writing them down, seeing them and thinking about them on the inside will help reinforce and identify key components necessary for dream destiny. Program yourself to work the plan for work dream achievement. I had to get a workout schedule, running, weight lifting and watching film. The result of dedication paid off and in 1982 I was voted captain of our team along with Michael Volpe and Marshal Grier.

I won all American Honor, All County, All State, All Area, and Most Valuable Player and WE WON TWO STATE CHAMPIONSHIP TOO.

1982 Captains: Marshal Grier, Tyrone Stowe, Michael Volpe

Tyronne Stowe with Childhood friend Craig Iron Head Heywood are presented State championship ring By Theresa Alaimo and Barabra Simbol.

Chapter 9

THE DECISION

The big pay-off is when, Dr. King's dream paid off and as a result Blacks were able to vote, segregated bath rooms, and separate restaurants, and separate schools no longer existed. Your dream will overturn an old generational curse or unproductive situation in your life! I can remember when Coach McPherson of Syracuse University came to Passaic High School. They liked me, but wasn't sure if I was a good fit for them. I went to visit but an offer for a scholarship was not made on the visit! The next college was The University of Cincinnati and they wanted me bad. Sometimes we get confused, by options, but narrowing out the options, by how bad do they want you, makes all the difference! Good deals work when both sides are happy and get what they want. My guide on this trip around the campus, was George Jamison. He was the big man on campus, and he was from Bridgeton, New Jersey! He was a good guy and showed me a good time. He played 12 years in the NFL too! Jamison was drafted in the 2nd round by the Detroit Lions.

When things are right, you should have a since of peace, a rest should be upon you that this is it, and I didn't feel Cincinnati was right for me. Are you at peace, where you are now in life? If not, keep moving! Don't stop moving until, you know you are in the right place! My next trip was to visit East Carolina! I'm a city boy, and we had to fly into one part of North Carolina and drive another 2 ½ or 3 hours to get to the school. I was done by the plane trip, and then the drive, all I kept thinking about was, if I came here, how long would it take me to get back home if I had to? I knew immediately this wasn't for me. After we reached the school, and met some of the players. The scariest sight you would ever want to see, was in the gym. The starting guard came up to me squeezed my hand and introduced himself to me, he said, "Hello I'm Terry Long" Terry Long! Terry was a power lifter and held the title of the strongest man or something of that nature. Between the flight, drive and Terry, my mind was made up, I had to get back home! Terry Long had a great career at East Carolina and he was drafted 4th round

Tyronne Stowe with girlfriend Elise Morgan. Now Elise Stowe.

by the Pittsburgh Steelers! Terry spent 8 years as a starting left and right guard! As I went back home, I knew home was where my heart was and I was in love with a young girl; named Elise Morgan from my home town. She and I have been married for over 25 years now. That is where my heart was and is to this day. We have four beautiful children Brittany, Tyrah, Zachariah and Samuel Stowe and six grand-children, Brielle, Brylen, Bryelle, Cayden, Carlin and Camryn. As I returned back home, I knew that Elise was waiting for me and so was Rutgers University! I had taken my last trip, Rutgers wanted me and I was their top player to recruit.

My weekend visit went great, and as they say, the rest is history! Michael Volpe and I both signed on to Rutgers University and Kevin Bryant signed to Delaware State University. My career as a student athlete at Rutgers

THURSDAY, FEB. 10, 1983

Photo by Mike Riccie

PASSAIC FOOTBALL PLAYERS (seated, left to right) Tyrone Stowe, Mike Volpe and Kevin Bryant sign scholarships while coach Tom Elsasser and Passaic High School principal Marjorie Bunnell look on. Stowe, a linebacker, and Volpe, a quarterback, signed full football scholarships for Rutgers. Bryant, a defensive halfback, will be attending Delaware State on a full scholarship.

Tyronne Stowe, Michael Volpe and Kevin Bryant sign College Scholarship.

was quite challenging. We were in an Independent Conference at that time of the Big East. The schedule was very, very tough. We were often out-manned by other talented Jersey-bred athletes who attended schools in other states. They were motivated to demonstrate their talents against the home team. The Scarlet Knights were facing jersey breed players going off to play for Penn State, West Virginia, and Boston College just to name a few. They didn't see the value in staying at home. I did and it was one of the greatest decisions of my life. I broke the starting line up as a freshman, and started for 4 years straight. Our game schedule was packed with matches against high-powered Division I schools like Penn State, University of West Virginia, Boston College, Pittsburgh, Syracuse and Temple.

SCARLET CO-CAPTAINS 1986
LEE GETZ   TYRONNE STOWE

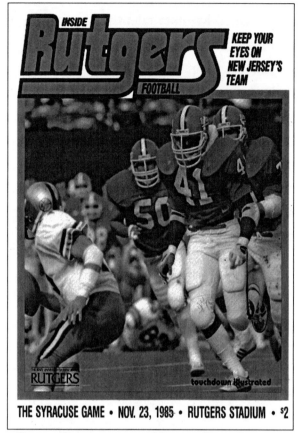

INSIDE

Rutgers
FOOTBALL

KEEP YOUR
EYES ON
NEW JERSEY'S
TEAM

RUTGERS

touchdown illustrated

THE SYRACUSE GAME • NOV. 23, 1985 • RUTGERS STADIUM • $2

Tyronne Stowe on cover of Rutgers Game Program.

At that time, Rutgers was struggling to establish its name as a winning school! During my time there, our best season was in 1986. We were 7-3 with hopes of a bowl bid. It was a major disappointment when the Army team was chosen over us. This was a hard pill to swallow as we beat Army that year and had a better record than them. They were 6-4 and we felt snubbed, and disrespected. We proved that we should have been there

All we needed were the lights of a Big Bowl Game to show the world that we were good. We had a goal to "change the old mastic," to remove the stuck-on residue of an old stubborn reputation, and begin a new legacy of winning. Apply this to your life. It is time for you to start building a new legacy in your own life. Decide right now to be a winner and work towards shedding past upsets and establishing new history. While at Rutgers University, I left my mark there! The home town boy did good!

Stowe among starters returning for Rutgers

College football

PISCATAWAY — Thirteen returning starters, including inside linebacker Tyronne Stowe of Passaic, will be on the field for the Rutgers football team's opener at the University of Florida on Saturday.

Seven members of the offense and six members of the defense will fill the same spots as in 1984's finale, a victory over Colgate that gave Rutgers a fulfilling 7-3 record.

The group has earned a combined total of 42 letters, including 19 to the offensive unit, where the backfield returns intact.

Defensively, junior Stowe and senior Roy Oake will line up at the inside linebacking posts and again are expected to be the team's top tacklers. Stowe (6-foot-2, 225) and Oake (6-2, 230) combined for 241 stops a year ago on their way to All-East honors. Stowe nailed 139 opposing runners while Oake stopped 124.

George Pickel (6-1, 235) and Tony Saguella (6-5, 265) are senior three-year letter-winners on the front line. Pickel, co-captain with Udovich, plays the same position as his brother Bill, a nose tackle for the Los Angeles Raiders. A second-team All-East pick last season, Pickel led the defensive linemen with 84 tackles.

He will be joined by his younger brother, Jim, a senior part-time starter last year, at the outside linebacking post.

The defensive backfield will be led by junior cornerback Steve Twamley and senior strong safety Jacque LaPrarie, the latter a former quarterback.

The offense is led by senior quarterback Rusty Hochberg, who

needs just five pass attempts, 35 completions and 30 yards to become the all-time Rutgers leader in those categories. Senior running back Albert Smith, meanwhile, has a chance at the all-time rushing mark and a record fourth rushing title.

Hochberg and Smith each have earned three letters.

Smith will be joined in the backfield by senior fullback Vernon Williams, also a three letter winner.

Necessary to the Knights' success are tackles Mike Brenner (junior, 6-0, 260) and Jim Keating (senior, 6-3, 240), and guards Clement Udovich (senior, 6-3, 240) and Lee Getz (senior, 6-3, 245). Brenner and Udovich, on the left side, have lettered three times. Keating and Getz, on the right, have two letters each.

New starters on the defense include, in addition to Jim Pickel, junior Harry Swayne (6-4, 250) and senior Paul Haloda (6-2, 233), both with some starting experience up front; and senior Darryl Brittingham and junior Jean Austin at the free safety and cornerback spots, respectively.

"It's been kind of scrambled eggs for a few days," said Rutgers head coach Dick Anderson about injuries that struck just before two-a-day practices came to a close with the beginning of classes. "I'm hoping everybody will be back by the end of the week."

File photo

TYRONNE STOWE (41) of Passaic makes a tackle during action last season against Syracuse. Stowe, an inside linebacker, is one of 13 returning starters for the Rutgers football team this season.

Tyronne Stowe Hit running back and forced fumble.

Making History- During my tenure from 1983- 1987 I was able to set records, and make history!

It was during my career at Rutgers University, with the help of great coaches and teammates that I was able to accomplish and establish myself in the history books of my University!

*Tyronne Stowe of Rutgers inducted into the Rutgers
Hall of Fame in 1998.*

*Tyronne Stowe of Rutgers University sacks
Florida Gator quarterback Kerwin Bell.*

Stowe was named AP All-American (HM) in 1985 and 1986.

1st-team AP All-East choice as an inside linebacker in 1985 and 1986, 1st- team All-ECAC choice in 1986

2nd team AP All-East selection in 1984.

Stowe was a two-time Homer Hazel Award winner as team MVP in 1985 and 1986 and was a 1986 Blue-Gray game participant. He holds the single game tackles mark with 27 vs. West Virginia in 1986 and is the Scarlet Knight career leader in tackles with 533. He also holds single season marks for total tackles (157 in 1985), assisted tackles (81 in 1986) and is second in unassisted tackles (106 in 1985). Stowe was inducted into the Rutgers University Hall of fame in 1998. My hope is that sharing my successful record will remind you that you've got to keep going- toward your own record of success and as you keep moving forward, remember that Matthew 7:7 encourages us to "Ask and it will be given to you; seek and you will find; knock and the door will be opened to you." There is a door, waiting to be opened by you, that will lead to your dream.

Don't give up until you find the right door! The text says that everyone who asks shall receive, seek and you will find, knock and the door will open! Keep seeking your dream and keep knocking. At some point, the door to your dream will open for you. How bad do you want it?

No one who knew me thought I would be a Division 1 player! Moreover, no one thought I would make history and break records. No one thought I was good enough, but they didn't know how bad I wanted it. I wanted it bad enough to make it happen. How bad do you want it?

Chapter 10

BEING AN OVER ACHIEVER

When people in my life called me an "over achiever," they were not insinuating that I was playing over my head and not that I was good enough to be there. What they were truly saying was that they never believed in my abilities to obtain my goals. Possess the wherewithal to live The Dream! To be called an over achiever in a condescending tone means someone is prejudging you and doesn't know what is really in you. If they knew your potential, they would have encouraged you to work harder to reach your goals. With that being said, don't become angry with people. People either don't know you, or they don't know what's on the inside of you! Just believe! Just believe in the dream and your belief will sustain your dream. No matter what comes or goes, you must believe, that you can achieve your dream.

Ponder these words: *only believe*. Mark 5:36 "Don't be afraid; just believe." A messenger for the synagogue official's house came and told him that his daughter was dead, Jesus told the official, do not be afraid any longer, only believe. You must learn to tune out fears, doubts, unbelief, and naysayers and only believe. Only believe that your dream will happen and you will achieve it. These two are words "Only Believe" are critical for Dream Success. The things you do on a regular basis will become part of your everyday life. The more you give yourself to the dream more it becomes part of you. Do not be afraid to trust in yourself and God. Your faith and God, are a winning combination.

I remember when the pro scouts came to Rutgers and watched film on me. I can remember listening, proud and feeling that they were talking about me. I listened on, only to hear something a dreamer doesn't need to hear, as they talked, I was on the other side of the room with partitions dividing us. I heard, "he is a pretty good player," but that I was a "question mark." They said, "He makes plays…" but in the same breath they questioned my size, my speed, and my strength, and ability to evolve into an NFL player. But what they did not know, and what they couldn't see was how bad I wanted to live my dream! I reminded myself, *only believe!* Do you understand why I keep bringing up the question, "How bad do you want it?" This is the question to ask yourself each day of your life. The things you are doing and pursuing are investments into your future. This focused activity of production answers the question; how bad do you want to achieve a particular goal or dream? Stop wasting time on vain, meaningless, unfruitful activity. Stop wasting your life, doing things that are incongruous with your dream's endeavors. How bad do you want to live your dream? My dream was to play professional football. What is your dream? What are you doing to bring it to pass? Are you living the dream? Are you working toward your dream? Have you already given up? Anyone can give up, but there are millions that can say, "I did it." Protect your dream!

You must be aware of dream killers! They are people, places and things that will try to discourage you from the dream that life has awaiting you! Be aware of your atmosphere. Avoid those dream killers and instead, surround yourself with supporters that agree with you! Matthew 18:19 says that, "if any two shall ask, it shall be done for them of my Father who is in Heaven." All you need is one person to believe with you in your dream. Together, with both of you seeking God and asking for the dream's manifestation, the dream shall be done! You need a partner to help you guard against discouragement and defeat. Does it seem like the dream will ever come to past? Your dream shall not die; your life will be a testimony to the world that dreams do come true. Your faith will keep the dream in perfect peace. Psalms 119:17 "I will not die but live, and will proclaim what the LORD has done." It is at these challenging times, that two are truly better than one. This idea is supported in Ecclesiastes. 4:10 "If either of them falls down, one can help the other up. But pity anyone who falls and has no one to help them up." Have you fallen into discouragement? Does it seem like the dream will never come to pass? Have you given up on your dream? Discouragement is a dream killer, and you need someone to help you recover from the falls of life's discouragements. I would like to resuscitate your dream. I know that it may have suffered great trauma. I know that the dream may have been existing lethargically and lean. Unless we surround ourselves with supporters, we find ourselves starving of resources, and spiritual proteins that produce healthy dreams. Sometimes, the dream may look like it is not breathing. Sometimes it looks like the dream is sick and malnourished. I want you to chew these words very slowly. I want to you to swallow these words, like medicine. I want you to allow it to digest inside of you to strengthen the dream spirit within you! Your dream is alive and well! I've come breathing air back into your dream. I'm administering compressions to save the life of your dream.

Your dream shall live and not faint. Your faith will keep the dream in perfect peace. You will see the goodness of your dream! Psalm 27:13 "I remain confident of this: I will see the goodness of the LORD in the land of the living." Sometimes things happen and disappointments and discouragement will set in and I want to tell you to adopt an achiever's attitude and fight to protect the dream. Sometimes, it may begin to look like this dream is impossible, but that is a part of the process. Living the dream is not going to be easy or happen instantly or come automatically. You must qualify for a unique, private, exclusive, club, of people living the dream. Most people will not live their dream, but you can and will- if you get up from wherever you are today and decide that every ounce of life left is focused on exercising perseverance, implementing steps toward your goal, and disciplining yourself to make your dream your reality! It's true, sometimes things don't go well, a job termination, a drug addiction, a period of incarceration. Your hardships may not be as extreme as these, or they may be more intense. Let me reiterate that hardship and challenge is part of the process. Am I saying that one must suffer and endure tough times in order to achieve the dream? Yes, that is exactly what I'm saying. Overcoming obstacles, opposition, and offenses is part of dream frame work. These obstacles came to bring out the best in you. The opposition comes to make you more than a conqueror! A conqueror is a person who subdues the problems that stand in their way. A conqueror is person that prevails to see manifestation. A conqueror is a person who has the will to take control of their destiny. A conqueror is a strong person that takes possession of something that others have. A conqueror is a person who wins no matter what he does! A conqueror is someone who gains victory by force of war. Does this describe you? Are you displaying the qualities of a conqueror? Are these attributes of a conqueror embedded within your character? These are traits that we must achieve, acquire possess and maintain. You are more than a conqueror; stand up, now and fight the good fight of faith where the victory is living the dream.

Chapter 11

DREAM PRESERVATION

want to introduce to you one of my hero's that many of you may already know. He is an athlete, motivational speaker and a true champion I hope his story reminds you that there is a champion inside of you and no matter what problems you are facing, you can still come out on top. Anthony Robles was a superstar wrestler at Arizona State University. In 2011, Robles won the 125 pound NCAA Division 1 wrestling title. Indeed this was a great feat for anyone, but what is so extra ordinary is Robles was born with one leg. This unique challenge pushed him to greatness! Due to what seemed like a disadvantage (having one leg and being unable to fight standing up), Robles had to force his opponents to the ground where his strengths lie, giving him a leg up on his competitors! Anthony Robles is a picture of allowing weakness to become strengths in order to become a champion. Anthony's life story speaks a strong answer to the question, "How bad do you want it?" Robles persevered and preserved his dream, when others in the same situation would have opted out. Be inspired to go where men have not been before and do what hasn't been done before. Be like Anthony Robles and preserve your dream despite the odds.

Dream preservation is the will to hold on to the dream in the face of opposition, antagonists, and atheistic doubters. When I use the term "dream preservation," I am referring to the will to hold on to the dream, adopting a habit of dream preservation keeps you working to make the dream happen. Dream preservation leads us to the answer to the question, "How bad do you want it?" How hard are you willing to fight to preserve the life of your dream? What do you do to save and preserve your dream when a setback occurs? Setbacks sometimes indicate that the time is not right, but setbacks are temporary hindrances that stop forward progress, and they don't have to be permanent! A setback gives you as a dreamer time to regroup, reorganize, reevaluate, and if necessary, a chance to do things differently. Setbacks give you an opportunity to come up with an improved plan. Preserve your dream by remembering to think optimistically. A setback can be a set-up, if we don't allow disappointment and discouragement to destroy the dream! Don't let the existence of temporary setbacks kill the dream. I come to bring new life back to your dream. Don't be discouraged, it is all part of the process. Keep your head up and be like that Timex watch, it takes a licking and keeps on dreaming!

Let me share with you how I struggled with disappointments and discouragement! It all started on Draft Night. The Draft Night I'm speaking about was the NFL Draft of 1987. I was projected to be picked in the 7th or 8th round. I had played in the Blue-Gray Football Classic and also in the Hula Bowl in Hawaii. I was an All American Honorable Mention too! I was excited about Draft Night and I just knew it was going to be the night of my dreams! However, that night turned out to be one of the longest nights of my life. My dream night turned into a nightmare! What was to be my draft dream night, turned into a nightmare! No NFL team called, to welcome me unto there team. I know I had paid my phone bill. My agent knew how to get in touch with me. I waited all day and all night, and my phone didn't ring. I didn't get drafted. I didn't get picked again! Here we are years later, I'm still not getting picked again, after determining that would never happen again in my life!

Are you still encountering something you said would never happen again? Are you still drinking? Are you still in debt? Are you still dreamless? What has happened, to discourage you from your dream? The draft night, was the day of great disappointment! I didn't get a call, but my friend and teammate, Big Harry whom was from South Philadelphia, got a call and was drafted by the Tampa Bay Buccaneers in the 7th round. I knew he would do well. Big Harry was about 6'5, 280 or 290 and could run. He was a basketball player too. Harry Swayne went on to do great things in the NFL. He's a Super Bowl Champion and played 14 years in the NFL. I was happy about Big Harry's success, but what about me? That was to be my night too. God what did I do wrong? Yes, I went there, but I'm not going to let you go that way. Don't turn on yourself and blaming yourself or God. God has a plan; it will come to pass another way! Mat 6:10 says, thy will, and not my will be done in earth as it is in Heaven. Take rest in God, God is going to do it another way.

2 Kings 5:1-14 There is great story in the Bible about a warrior named Naaman, captain of the army of the king of Aram, was a great man with his master, and highly respected, because by him the LORD HAD given victory to Aram. The man was also a valiant warrior, but he was a leopard. He defeated a town or a city and he takes a young

girl into his home to wait on His family as a servant. They treated her well and she became close to them and grew to love them. And if I can just say, if you can't love the one you want, learn to love the ones you are with. Well she saw Naaman living with leprosy. She lived in Israel seen the miracles and many people getting healing done by the prophets. Something inside her promoted her to share her faith with her master! If you don't learn to share with others, what you have, your dream will not come true. The prophet didn't come out to meet him, he didn't invite you in the house. He didn't come out and wave his hands over your head and hand to heal you. God was going to do it another way.

The Bible teaches this principle in Galatians 6:7- Do not be deceived, God is not mocked, for whatever a man sows, this he will reap. This young girl could have got mad, about being a slave, taken from her home, and no family to love. But she made the best out of a bad situation. She kept a good attitude, she realized they could have killed her. They spared her life and she was thankful.

She was happy or she kept a positive outlook on life. They saw her as part of the family. She sowed a seed of humanity, how can you see someone sick and not want to help make them well? She said, if my master would just go see the prophet, you will be healed. It's too many of us believers not being healed from past hurts in life. It's causing us to walk with a limp and we can't walk up right before God. The King of Aram send a letter to the King of Israel, He panic and wondering why the king of Assyria is picking on him, the King replies; Who am I God, God but you should be an extension of God in the world. The king tore his clothes and called a fast. The Prophet Elijah said, no problem King send the man to me. Naaman comes and the preacher doesn't answer the door, He sent his servant to the door and tells him to go wash in the Jordan River and dip seven times! Naaman walked away mad, 1.- because the Prophet didn't meet and greet Him. 2.- He didn't invite you into the house 3.- He didn't come out and wave His hands over your head and hand to heal you, God was going to do it another way. Naaman walked away mad, a Commander not understanding that the orders you follow will determine the victories one enjoys. Naaman started reasoning in his mind, and stopped living by faith. Someone in his company spoke and said, Sir, the prophet told you to do a simple thing, like say I'm sorry, forgive me, thank You for being here, I need you, I can't make it without you, I love you. The Prophet told you to do an easy thing, what is so hard that we can't do the easy things now, our hearts are hard. The girl loved him enough to tell him to go see the Prophet. The King loved him enough to write the letter. The group that traveled with you loved you enough to go and protect you on the journey. The prophet loved you enough to tell you what to do. And Naaman walks away mad because God healing him another way.

As he was walking away someone had enough faith to speak, to turn the mad commander around and to bring him back to His dream of being healed. Naaman travel all that way for a purpose. He came all that way for healing, just to give up and walk away in pride and self- presumption. God is about to heal you another way, don't limit God, stop trying to understand God. Just stand under His words. Compliance is the key to completion. What needs to be completed in your life? Complete the process, do what is ask of you and see the harvest return and bless your life.

Naaman swallowed His pride and His ideas and obeyed the instructions told Him from the Prophet. My father, had the prophet told you *to do some* great thing, would you not have done *it?* How much more *then,* when he says to you, 'Wash, and be clean'?" So he went down and dipped *himself* seven times in the Jordan, according to the word of the man of God; and his flesh was restored like the flesh of a little child and he was clean. Romans 11:33–O the depth of the riches both of the wisdom and knowledge of God! how unsearchable are his judgments, and his ways past finding out! Isiah- 55:8-9– For my thoughts are not your thoughts nor are your ways, my ways, declare the Lord. For as the heaven are higher than the earth so are my ways higher than your ways. And my thoughts than your thoughts. God is going to do it another way!

That Draft night turned into the longest night of my Life! I was so upset. I was crushed and heartbroken, the dream seemed over. I got into an argument Elise, my girlfriend, now wife, and she screamed, "don't get mad at me because you didn't get drafted!" She was right, her shout sobered me up, and I wasn't even drinking. Her words cleared my head. She helped me get a grip on the reality of my situation. Elise was my biggest fan. She was at every game, rain, sleet or snow and was there for me through high school and college.

We must be very careful, at times of disappointments that we don't take out our frustrations on our loved ones. Those who are closest to us usually take the brunt of our unwarranted frustration. We tear our support down, by fighting and shattering the relationships intended to build us up. At times of disappointment, we have to deal with the hurts and pains without inflicting hurt and pain on others. Knowing that somewhere at the end of the rainbow, there is pot of gold full of dreams waiting for us!

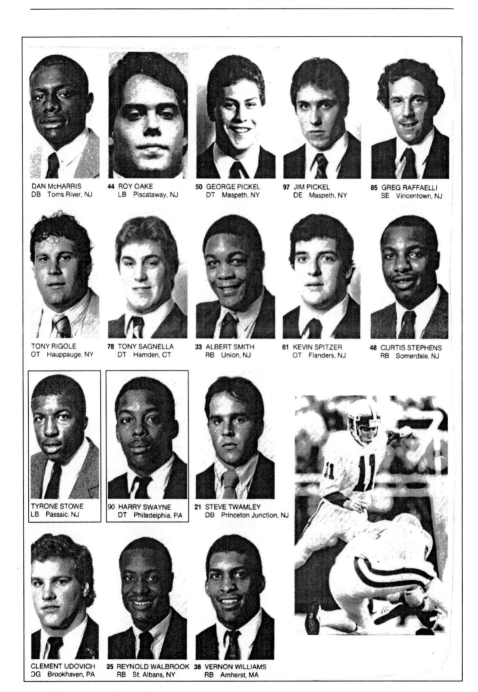

DAN McHARRIS
DB   Toms River, NJ

44 ROY OAKE
LB   Piscataway, NJ

50 GEORGE PICKEL
DT   Maspeth, NY

97 JIM PICKEL
DE   Maspeth, NY

85 GREG RAFFAELLI
SE   Vincentown, NJ

TONY RIGOLE
OT   Hauppauge, NY

78 TONY SAGNELLA
DT   Hamden, CT

33 ALBERT SMITH
RB   Union, NJ

61 KEVIN SPITZER
OT   Flanders, NJ

48 CURTIS STEPHENS
RB   Somerdale, NJ

TYRONE STOWE
LB   Passaic, NJ

90 HARRY SWAYNE
DT   Philadelphia, PA

21 STEVE TWAMLEY
DB   Princeton Junction, NJ

CLEMENT UDOVICH
OG   Brookhaven, PA

25 REYNOLD WALBROOK
RB   St. Albans, NY

38 VERNON WILLIAMS
RB   Amherst, MA

Tyronne Stowe and Harry Swayne with some of our college teammates.

71

Whenever you get bucked off the horse, get right back on it! Pick up the pieces of the dream. Yes, the dream has been shattered but in the shattered state, the dream still exists. It will take greater effort now to gather the shattered pieces, and methodically begin to assemble the dream again like a puzzle. All the pieces of the dream are still in your hands. Begin to build the dream again by putting the dream back together and at this point, take a little more time and effort. You have to face the facts of life and determine that no matter what happens, your dream will succeed. Don't throw yourself a pity party, get up out of the cloud of doubt and depression. Brush the dirt off of yourself, wash your face, and pick up the pieces. Start all over, from right where you are, and build the dream! I wish I could go back and give my younger self the advice I'm giving you. The next morning, I didn't want to get out of bed, those cuts to my feelings were still bleeding, and I was still bandaging up my wounds. The NFL teams were calling and I was still hurting, but happy to receive their calls, even though the calls were a day too late and hundreds of thousands of dollars too short. They called, but I asked, "Why didn't you call me yesterday if you wanted me?" I was still so wounded by the disappointment. Please let this caution you. Don't allow the disappointment to stop you from your appointment! How bad do you want it?

The 1987 NFL Draft was definitely a great year for linebackers. The competition to get drafted was fierce and the pool of talent was great. Competition is not bad, and it gives you a good assessment of where you are, and it pushes you to where you need to be. But when you understand true competition, it really brings the best out of you. It's not really about competition between each other, it is about us completing our individual assignments in life. It's about us all

72

completing the dream. The world would be a better place if each one of us understood the purpose of dream and goal setting. In 1987 the deck was stacked with good and great linebackers! Cornelius Benet, Mike Junkin, Shane Conlans, Brian Bosworth, Johnny Holland, Alex Gordon, Rick Graf, Ray Berry, David Wyman, Winston Moss, David Brandon, Todd Howard, Onzy Elam, Michael Brooks closes out the 3rd of the NFL. Other notable names of this draft year were my friends and former teammates Hardy Hardware Nickerson, 5th round pick of the Steelers and Greg "Can't Avoid the Lloyd" 7th round pick of the Pittsburgh Steelers!

The next day walking around campus, I was bombarded with questions. "Why didn't you get drafted?" "What happened?" I simply answered, "I don't know." I felt depressed, upset and disappointed. I felt like I had let my family and friends down. Life is not easy, and it is often unpredictable. Things happen and everybody has a different road to travel. You have to protect the dream at times like this. Stay focused in mind, body and spirit! Proverbs 18:14 poses the question: "But a broken spirit who can bear?" Your spirit is the inner unseen you. It's the new person you are called to be. We must work to preserve a positive, united spirit, in the mist of distractions that come to disassemble our hearts. Don't let life break the heart of your dream. It's at these breaking points that you have to just hold on! It's at these breaking points that you must not allow a break down! Some people commit suicide over bankruptcy, foreclosures, and debt. I'm telling you to hold on to your dream. Don't make a permanent decision over temporary setbacks. Don't allow anything to break down the dream. You are neither the first nor the last person to face such situations and setbacks and you can come out on top! How bad do you want it? Hold on to the dream! Even in the midst of any problems or disappointments you may face, hold on to those things that are lovely. Hold on to whatsoever things are of good reports. Keep virtue, keep praise. Keep your mind on these things. That's what we are told to do in Philippians 4:8. "Finally, brothers and sisters, whatever is true, whatever is noble, whatever is right, whatever is pure, whatever is lovely, whatever is admirable—if anything is excellent or praise-worthy—think about such things." Keep your mind on your dream! Free Agent- Don't let the world cause you to stay captive. Stay a free in your mind and keep moving forward in the dream. In spite of disappointments and discouragements don't let the world cause you to captive, stuck, or dreamless. Get free today to do what has not been done before. I want to share with you a story. His name is Jebez and the story is found in 1 Corinthians 4, the sons of Judah were Perez, Hezron, Cami, Hur and Shobal.

It was the family of praise, and as life moved forward praise turning to frustration. Praise became hard and the weight of life became too heavy. Life was drying up the praise, and it's at the hard times like this someone has to have the courage to change, the course of life. In verse 9-Jabez was more honorable than his brothers. Yet his mother named him Jabez. My mother called me every big head joke one could think of and it took away confidence from me, I was always thinking that I was not good enough. Name calling is not permitted in my House. Because I know the pain of what calling name can do. The name calling was an innocent attempt to disciple me, but all it did was divide me, and weaken my eternal value. The Bible says because she bore Him in pain. I'm not sure what my mom was going through the years of speaking hurtful names. I wonder what life would have been like if Jabez's mother would have named him, Wonderful or Brilliant and not pain. Every time she called him she was reminded of the pain and the old feels from yester year would come back and its pain would cause us to feel the hurts and pains of the past all over again. Know this hurt people hurt people. You were born to praise, you are from the tribe of praise, Life comes to challenge, test and strengthen our faith. But then something goes wrong, someone steals your business, someone walks out on you, someone dies, you break your arm and the dream is unconceivable. All is left is pains and regrets. All that is left is questions and uncertainty. Jabez was more honorable than the rest of His family- Jabez was honest enough to examine Himself and saw that something is wrong. God made me to be a Praiser, and a Trail blazer and why am I stuck. I'm a praiser not a complainer! Jabez knew something had to change. 1st Chronicles 4:10- Now Jabez called on the God of Israel, I challenge you to call on God today. I challenge you to get back to praising God. I challenge you to go to God with you pains. I challenge you to go to God with your hurt. Ask God to heal you. Ask God to turn this situation around.

Ask Him to bless you and your Dream. Ask God to enlarge my borders and that Your hand might be with me, and that You would keep *me* from harm that *it* may not pain me!" So that I could live the dream you were ordained to live for life! And God granted him what he requested. God will grant you your request, it's not over. It's not too late. It's just getting started. God is granting now your request.

Keep your mind on your dream! Free Agent- Stay free in your mind to dream. In spite of disappointments and discouragements don't let the world cause you to be captivated, stuck, or dreamless.

Not being drafted meant that I was free to sign with any team I thought would give me the best opportunity to be successful. I had a few teams interested in me, like the Pittsburgh Steelers, San Diego

Chargers and the Dallas Cowboys, along with a handful of others. My favorite team was the Dallas Cowboys, but I was also interested in my home teams, the New Jersey Giants and the New York Jets. But the reality of me making it onto a team as free agent was almost impossible. Do you understand the odds of me being a lawyer were better than the odds of me becoming a professional football player? Understand that many times, just like in my situation, the odds will not be in your favor and the cards may be stacked against you. Are you a betting man? Do you feel lucky? Are you willing to go all in, for your dream? Will you ante up to receive the purse after winning and achieving your dream? Let me paint the picture of how high the cards were stacked against me as a free agent. The veterans had already made their impacts and contributions to the team. They have already made a name for themselves. They have already formed relationships with the coaches, owners and players. Then add to the mix all the new draft picks, with those big signing bonuses. The coaching staffs, scouts, and front office have already invested hours of research and money making their choices. After giving their stamp of approval, it's hard to change their minds with so little time! And here I come, a free agent, rejected initially, standing on a dream and a prayer. The chances of a free agent making a team are slim to none. Well I want you to know that the combination of those two things- a dream and a prayer- work pretty good together! I found hope and learned a lesson that I want to share with you. Being a free agent allows us to stay free and our minds remain free to dream. In spite of disappointments and discouragements don't let the world cause you to be captive, stuck, or dreamless.

I signed a free agent contract with the San Diego Chargers and I was going to Cali-forn-I-A! Dan Fouts was the quarter back, with Gary Anderson was the running back and Hall of famer to be Kelvin Winslow was there, wow! On the defensive side of the ball were Billy Ray Smith, Gill Bird, Chip Banks, and Gary Plummer. And here comes a new kid on the block, an un-drafted free agent dreaming and praying for a spot on the team. I was waiting for an opportunity to show them that I could play. I practiced well during the preseason. I played the 1st game special teams only. The second game, I played special team and 5 snaps at Inside linebacker I made 2 tackles and the third game, I just played special teams. I went to the coach and talked to him after about playing in the last game. The final pre-season game before the last cut! I knew this game was crucial, for this was the game, before the regular season started.I was close, but they already had plans to let me go! I didn't even get a chance to play, to determine my fate. Some things in life, you can't control, just know it's not over yet. In the words of Jessie Jackson, "keep hope alive!" The next morning, a thunder of a knock banged on my door. The voice said, Coach wants to see you and bring your play book! Wow, for a football player, a dreamer, you don't ever want that knock on your door! I felt that I wasn't given a fair chance? Well the truth of the matter is, you may not have been given a fair chance, but you were given a chance. Things in life will not always be fair, but will you be ready to maximized, the little opportunities and make it big out of them! I missed out on my chance by being "okay," ordinary and average, not eye-catching. During the few shots I had to show the coaches and the team, I didn't do enough to change their opinions of me. I failed to sway their appraisal of my abilities!

Getting cut wasn't a new term to me, I was familiar with getting cut from the streets. But getting cut, from the team, left a scar that is still there to this day. I returned home as the hometown hero, that was close, but didn't make it! I returned home, as the one that could have, but didn't make it! I came home and had to answer questions again. How come you got cut? How come you didn't make it? I knew that I had some tough decisions to make. Do I hold on the dream, or cuff it? A few years back, basketball superstar LeBron James had a television special called "The Decision." LeBron James was so good he came right out of High School and went to the Pro's! LeBron was the franchise player of the Cleveland Cavaliers. After reaching the playoffs for the first time since 1992, the Cavaliers were fighting for respect as a franchise. Even with LeBron's leadership, the Cavaliers came short, year after year in the play offs! LeBron was with Cleveland for 6 years, but he never could win the big one. LeBron, Rookie of the Year, Olympic Gold Medalist, NBA All Star, MVP, Scoring Champion, "The King" was, essentially, without a crown! LeBron James, "The King," was Championship Ring-less! After years of coming short of the dream, LeBron made a decision to leave the Cavaliers and join the Miami Heat in pursuit of his dream.

What big decision do you need to make? What do you have to do to make the dream a reality? Is it time for you to move? Is it time for you to change teams, or are you just used to losing? Are the decisions you're making supporting your dream? The decisions you make dictate the direction your dream will take! People hate LeBron James now, today because he left the team to follow the dream. But I want you to know, that this wasn't about the team. It was all about LeBron's dream. His dream is to win a championship and dreams will take you places! I was faced with a LeBron-like decision in my life too. My decision was not televised, not viewed by millions of people, but it was a defining moment in my life that had its ramifications to my dream. It was me and the dream against discouragement, wrestling to see how bad I wanted my dream to live. So there I was, at home after getting cut, spending time with my daughter Brittany and working at Passaic High School.

The decision I had to make was, to stay in faith and believe in God for a door to open. Faith I get from my mother, she made us go to church and I'm so glad she did! I owe my mother Marva special thanks for showing me the way to Jesus. She is a fighter literally she would fight at the drop of the hat, she has used this inner strength to fight off cancer for about 5 rounds, and by the grace of God she was undefeated at age 70. That "never give up" spirit was passed down to me from my mom. With a church background, I learn about God, don't let the world steal him away from you! I loved God and church. I sang on the choir, want to hear a song? No, just kidding. I was brought up in the church and I stayed involved in all the festival activities. Faith kept the dream and the prayer alive. Elise and I, made the decision to keep the dream alive. And I want to encourage you to make the decision to keep the dream and a prayer alive! I did it! LeBron James did it, and now it's your turn. Decide today to follow the dream! Make the decision to pursue your dream! LeBron went to South Beach to play for the Miami Heat! He went there to give new life to his dream. LeBron took a giant step forward toward his dream making it to the Championship Round to battle Dallas Mavericks then winning his Championship rings two years, back-to-back. LeBron got closer to his dream, and now your dream is getting closer to you now also keep moving forward to the dream because New Life is in the dream.

Don't get stuck in unproductive activity, make sure to keep moving forward in the direction of the dream. There is an inner navigation system inside of you, so follow the directions, trust the path, and you will end up at your dream destiny! I made a decision to work out very hard in preparation for next opportunity! If opportunity knocked on your door right now, would you be ready for it? Why not? This is the chance you have been waiting for. This is the chance of a life time. This chance might be your last!

Chapter 12

A TIME FOR PREPARATION!

It's time for preparation! Get ready for your Dream! Your next audition, next interview, next evaluation, is your next opportunity coming back around! I can feel it, as you read this book, this time you'll be ready and you will seize the moment! Preparation is when opportunity and action meet! Let me encourage you now, as you are reading this book, you must come into agreement with your dream. People, places and things are lining up for you to make your dream a reality! Be bold and make a decision today, and let your dream live! I kept working out, kept believing; kept fighting the good fight of faith! You will win and the prize is the dream of a lifetime! Do it today to let your dream live, the rest of your life! LeBron's decision has since paid off, his preparation, hard work and willingness to chase his dream has manifested. The Miami Heat won back to back championships in 2012 and 2013, and LeBron James was MVP. His decision brought dream success. Make a decision, how bad do you want it?

The Strike-of 1987

The NFL Strike of 1987, was new life for my dream. My mental preparation paid off for me. When I was writing this book the NFL strike had just ended, and the NFL owners and the NFL player have just settled the strike. The teams were arriving to training camp. A settlement had been reached, football is back and the 2011 season is on. For the next decade football is secure. I was so happy to hear that the strike is over. Nobody wins, when there is a strike! I was even happier to hear, that the older players will receive some financial compensation as a result of this new contract! Thank You Jesus! The game does owe the older players, their due. The game had evolved on the backs of our Forefathers of Football. Everybody in football isn't rich. It sure hurts to be a part of something, and you can't afford to take your family, to see a game you love so much. The owners now, have to split a certain percentage of revenue and it was not always like that in the past. In 1987 the players staged a strike also! A Strike is when people don't go to work to get better wages and benefits. But by me keeping the dream and a pray alive, I went to work for a wage and got some benefit due to the strike of 1987! I understood what the players were doing and felt they needed to strike, and I felt that I had to cross the life of the strike to fight for my dream. I felt like this was the second chance, I had been waiting for! The strike was an opportunity for me, for I had a few strikes against me already! I was broke, unemployed and dreamless! I had some strikes against me, but the dream was still alive! Growing up as children, do you remember being challenged by someone to cross the line? They would say something like if you are bad enough cross this line.

I want to challenge you: the line in the sand has been drawn, you are on the other side of the line, I dare you to cross every line that separates you from living the dream on the other side of the line lies the new you! On the other side of the line, is the dream! Will you cross the line to get what the dream has for you? Strike time, was the right time for me, timing is everything, and knowing when to move is essential. This was my time to strike into action! I decided to sign a new contract with the Pittsburgh Steelers and the dream was resurrecting. I felt I had to cross the line of the strike to fight for my dream. I reported to training camp, with much security and fan fair, like a rock star. I reported to camp under police patrol as escorts, guard dogs, and wild fans and foes. Wow, how quick life can change, I was just home with my daughter babysitting, now I got police escorts, guard dogs, and crazy fans. Do you know that you are only a minute away from a turn around, in your life? Hold on to the dream, cross the line of opposition everything will be fine! But I was living the dream it didn't matter to me. Remember if you don't mind, it doesn't matter. Stay focused on where you're going, stay focused on your dream. Did I mention, the line I crossed was the picket line? The police and their dogs were there to protect us from the thousands of people picking, screaming at us, and calling us scabs. Some people were spitting on us, and a few screaming matches, a few altercations broke out. But I was living the dream! The strike, I believe was ordained from my personal prayer request. I know that sounds a little bit over the top to think that God would create a strike in one of the biggest sports arena just for me. But you must have confidence that when you pray, God hears you and whatsoever we ask we know that we have the petitions that we desire of him – 1John 15:5. Wow, I was on the Pittsburgh Steelers Team! The 5-time Super Bowl Champion Pittsburgh Steelers. A dream and a prayer go a long way! Hall of fame Coach Chuck Noll was the Head

Coach and our defensive coordinator was Coach Tony Dungy! Our defensive line Coach was no other that Mean Joe Green! Just going to the stadium was electrifying. Just looking around on the wall and seeing the rich history, made you feel like you're a winner! The success of the organization made you feel like you were part of it! We played about 5 games under the strike season, then the strike ended, and the real players came back! Are you a real player? Do you possess what it takes to play with the Big Boys? If not, just stay on the porch then! Under this new agreement, the teams were able to keep five players from the strike on their rosters.

I can remember them all, we have a great fidelity together; It was Brian Blankenship, Larry Griffin, Cornell Gowdy, Joey Clinkscales, and the dreamer Tyronne Stowe! We were fortunate to make the Team Roaster! But we had to earn our respect, by playing up to NFL caliber! We all made great contributions to the Team.

A great saying in football is the film doesn't lie, with this means either you are you doing things properly and getting the job done or you're not! What is the film saying about your life? Are you getting the Job done? Are you doing things properly? Are you making a contribution to your team, career, friends and family? Over time we were integrated into being part of the team, I was a Special Teams stand out! Whatever you do, make it special to you. Knowing what you do, is just as important as knowing what you don't do well! I want to take a little time to say, thank you to Coach Chuck Noll for believing in me. Giving me a second and a third chance to play and live my Dream. Coach has passed since this book was started, and to All of Coach Noll's family bless you all he was a great man.

Chapter 13

AWAKEN FROM THE DREAM

After making it, I felt the hurdles were over, but maybe I got comfortable and let my guard down on my dream, maybe this is how things were to be. My good friend, Greg Lloyd, was on injured reserve due to a knee problem, they activated him and deactivated me! Here we go again.... Do you feel like the rug keeps getting pulled from underneath you again? Well that is exactly how I felt, being cut twice in one year, by two different teams, maybe this is the furthest I was meant to go. Battling in one's own mind, going back and forth about what to do sometimes causes a loss of confidence. You know they say, "three strikes and you're out," but thank God that's in baseball. Again, I was back at stay at home dad, jobless and dreamless! I had the chance to taste the dream, but I didn't even get my feet wet in it! Mental depression was now setting in, and the roller coaster ride of the dream got the best of me, I was worn out and doubts were setting in. Maybe babysitting was best for me! We know that is not true, but sometime things will get the best of you!

I was watching Brittany sleeping as if she had not a care in the world, my world was totally opposite and the question came to me, as I sat, in pity, that same old question: "How bad do you want it?" But now it was as if my daughter was asking me, "How bad do you want it for me daddy"? I looked at her and knew that taking care of her and her Mother was my purpose, and football was the vehicle to do that! Elise was working, and I wanted her to have a different life. They were depending on me, it's true: what you are doing will affect others! Faith rose up within me and I was determined to keep believing! I stayed ready, anticipating something good happening for me! Within weeks, Pittsburgh called me back! An anchor performance was the order of the day. The Pittsburgh Steelers called me back because they wanted to see more of me.

If at first you don't succeed try, try again, never stop trying to make opportunities your occupation! Your preparation will pay off! Get ready, for a call back. I returned, to Pittsburgh with a chip on my shoulder, to prove that I should be on the team. You must be a part of a team, because nobody can make it on their own. I finished the year out, with good special team success! The following seasons, I was established and living the dream. The hunger for success had diminished, and I took the dream for granted! We went to the play offs two years and things were good for the underdog, undrafted free agent dreamer. This is what happens to most of us, we want to be married, we want to have children, we want a new car or home, but unsure about everything! I had developed, a worldly mind set, that I might as well let the good times last. I might as well enjoy it while it lasted. I could be here today, and back home tomorrow! The NFL stands for, Not For Long! So I might as well live it up, but I was letting myself down, I stopped dreaming and started spiraling down. This is what happens, when you reach a plateau and don't have any other goals.

Tyronne Stowe with Steeler teammates, a night out on the Town. Arron Jones, Darren Jordan, Hardy Nickerson, Greg Lloyd, David Little and Bryan Hinkle

An unappreciative attitude sets in, and the dream starts drifting away. If you don't keep striving for more, you will give less and never gain. The vision has gotten distorted, the party scene was leading me down the wrong streets! The hard truth is that many of us do this. After you have reached a goal, how long did it take before you began to take things for granted? What did you want, and work for, but now take for granted?

How is your marriage? The new car you brought? How about your health, are you in shape? Yes, I am in shape, round! In life, because of our humanistic nature, we take what we have for granted! The city of Pittsburgh is a party place and being a Pittsburgh Steeler living the dream didn't make things any easier. The Black and Gold uniform presented temptations, and tests that I failed royally! I wasn't well developed in these new areas of testing. The city of Pittsburgh was not the problem; my lack of discipline was the problem. Some people can't handle the dream life. Responsibility comes with success. I had the break through, I made the team, I was living the dream. A false sense of security sets in, right along with the party life! I lacked and needed maturity and discipline. I over indulged in the party scene and I was waking myself up from the dream. I did my share of partying this and almost cost me the dream. They had the greatest after parties, all night long. I fell to the sex, drugs and rock and roll which came in a package. Many fall because of this package and it sends you packing. Every day the dream was fading away. I failed a drug test. I was jeopardizing the dream. I risked my family's future as I was out of control, living my life wildly, and letting the good times roll with dream-shattering activities.

Chapter 14

AMAZING GRACE

C oach Chuck Noll, in all his greatness, came to my room, looked me in the eyes, and said that he was greatly disappointed with me. When I took an honest look, I realized I was disappointed with myself. This Hall of Fame coach thought enough about me to come my room and care enough about my well-being. I'd like to say thank you, to Coach Knoll again, for the third chance, but this one was redemptive. He gave me a chance, to get myself together

TYRONE STOWE

Tyronne Stowe Sitting in uniform
Ready to play!

and showed me amazing grace. Yes, I messed up and you might have messed up too, but get yourself together right now and take full responsibility for your wrongs and man up! Stop going down the wrong street and get back to the dream and to following the dream.

Don't risk losing everything, it's not worth it! He lifted me up. "Go back home to your wife, my brother. Go back home to your children's mother. Don't risk drinking and driving. You will kill the dream. Don't risk a few meaningless moments of lust ruin your home! Don't risk the dream!" Those words marked a turnaround. Coach Chuck Noll has passed since this book has been released. To the Noll family and the entire Steeler Nation, I want to say that I love you for giving me a third chance to live my dream. From the bottom of my heart, I express my thanks to the Steeler organization, and I, Tyronne Stowe, am today and forever grateful for you giving me a third chance. Thank you, thank you, thank you! You could've cut me, replaced me, filled my position with anybody! Thank you, to Coach Noll again, for giving me this chance. This act of mercy, sobered up my life. I haven't had a beer, or party stick or etc. in over 24 Years. to stop? Are you putting the dream at risk? The things we are doing today have long term effects! I played 4 years with the Pittsburgh Steelers. Under Coach Noll's leadership we had

Drugs not part of dream for Stowe

(Continued From Page 1)

back that a lot of people called to complain (about his being waived)," Stowe related. "I had a nice following. That made me feel real good."

Everything he received, Stowe said, started with education.

"It's a foundation to work with," he said. "You are building a foundation for life. Education you have for the rest of your life. You may get knocked down, but it shines beyond anything.

"Put some time in (to study)," Stowe urged the youngsters. "I put in just a couple of hours a day, even an hour a day, and it showed. You will see a difference in your marks."

Drugs will put a damper on any aspirations, however, he said.

"Drugs are killing society," said Stowe, dressed in a gray suit. "Say no to drugs and alcohol. Be a clean person, a wholesome person. It will work, I guarantee it.

"Why make a mistake and then learn?," he asked. "Why go through a hassle to learn?"

Stowe's message, along with those of counselor Ricky Smith — John's brother — and the patient, identified only as Terence, reached at least some of the youngsters interviewed following the speech. Fourth graders like Joe McCoy, William Perna, Sammy Alvarez, Reece Carter and Jeanna Clanton all agreed using drugs was of no value.

"You can be cool and not use drugs," said Alvarez, 10.

Added Carter, also 10, in response to Stowe's dedication, "It takes a lot of work to be a football player."

Fifth graders Tuonor Grier, Manuel Audujer and Robert Griffin concurred with their younger schoolmates.

"If you use them, you get addicted and you're hooked for the rest of your life," said Grier, 10.

The kids' views were in line with what Stowe wanted to get across.

"Hopefully, I opened up a couple of eyes," he said. "Then the next time someone talks, we'll get a couple more. If we got one out of the whole thing, it was worth it.

"I'm not a great speaker," Stowe concluded, "but it doesn't count when the cause is right."

Tyronne Stowe speaking to a group about making bad decisions playoff appearances, and we made it to the Division Championship. John Elway went to work on us after having a 14- 0 lead at half time. But playing for the Steelers was great fun, and I was living the dream.

During those good old days, I met some of Football's Hero's that I had as teammates and friends. Dewayne Woodruff, John Star worth, Donny Shell, Luis Lips, Robin Cole, Brian Hickle, David Little and Mike Webster were a few of those hero's. I can remember the first time I knocked Mike down, I felt bad as I was in my prime and his better days had come and gone already. That has been a chip on my shoulder ever since- proving myself to all doubters. You can make it through the gauntlet of life and make your dream happen! Do you want it bad enough?

Tyronne Stowe making a tackle on Philadelphia Eagels
running back Keith Byars

Chapter 15

ONE PLAY AWAY!

I'd like to pause and just encourage you that you are one play away from living the dream! Yesterday may have been bad, but today is another play. Each day you live to see, you get another chance to make things happen! While playing for the Steelers, I made a name for myself as a Special Team Specialist! I was the Captain for Special Teams and Coach George Stewart was our Special Team Coach. Coach Stew would get excited, and that got us excited. On our schedule was the big Monday Night Football Game! We were facing the Los Angeles Rams at that time! And everybody was excited because it was Monday Night Football! Everybody watches Monday Night football! During the second half we kicked off the ball, and all I could see was a man come through this little hole, he was stuck with nowhere to run. I met him face to face, this was my strength! And as the Gap Band would say, "You dropped the bomb on me!" Yes, I did and on Monday Night Football! My cell phone didn't stop ringing everybody saw the Big Monday Night Knockout! It was poetry in motion, a beautiful site to see! Robert Delpino, the kick returner at impact, was, as we say, "asleep." The crowd roared when he fumbled the ball due to the crush of the thunderous hit. That roar sounded good! I still get excited about it today.

The dream, and the goals you will reach will have you smiling for a life time. How bad do you want it? I hit the returner so hard, he was knocked out and suffered a concussion. The Rams took a time out and the network went to two commercial breaks for delay of the game. Delpino had to be taken out on a stretcher! Honestly, I'm not happy about what happened to him, but I was happy that everyone saw I belonged in the NFL! I was happy because people were talking about me, the undrafted, twice cut, three time looser, baby sitter, undisciplined partier living the dream! Football is a rough sport. Did you hear that? I discovered my strength you must stop majoring on your weakness and find your strengths. The key to your greatness is in your strengths! Work on improving your weakness in an effort to accentuate your strengths! The Monday night knock out that everyone saw was the one play turned my life around!

Understand that you are just one play way away from turning your whole life around! You are one act away from seeing your dreams come true. 1 Samuel 17 – David was a nobody, the baby of the family and his father sent him as a delivery boy, to bring his brother a pizza, bread and cheese. But when he got there the chance of his dreams was standing in front of him. It was a big giant named Goliath. What is the name of the giant standing in your way? Cancer, stroke, depression, or divorce whatever it may be, know that this day might be the day your life changes. Know that today, might be the day the dream takes form. David's dream was to be King. This single action of defeating Goliath gave him entrance to the Palace! Are you ready, to enter into the palace of your dreams? Keep this in mind always, you could be only a day away from your dream! You are one play away from your future. You are one day away from your dream job. You are one phone call away from the big deal. You are one day away from victory. You are one day from being royalty. You are one day away from your breakthrough! Shout breakthrough! Let out the frustration and say, "Breakthrough!" You have been separated for success, this is your time for a breakthrough, shout breakthrough! No more walls stand between you and your dream. The walls are coming down and you are going up!

Please close your eyes and see yourself going up, see yourself making the big play and see yourself making a difference, see yourself making the big play. See yourself closing the big deal! Please, again close your eyes and see yourself strong, empowered, and able to do whatever it takes to live the dream. How bad do you want it?

Chapter 16

SHINING IN THE SUN!

S hining at the right time is pivotal! Are you ready for your time
to shine in the sun? I was offered, a new contract by the Phoenix
Cardinals and I was going to Arizona, to shine in the sun. My special
team play is what brought me to the Cardinals and I finally made
some money too (that never hurts). I was a starving Pro Football
player during those first four years and I couldn't wait for the breakthrough. My dream was awaiting for me in the Valley of the Sun. I
had established myself as a quality Special Teams player, but the fullness of the dream of this undrafted, slow, not athletic, free agent was
to be a starting player in the NFL! As I came to Arizona, it became
my Promised Land and I fell in love with the place, and with God
like never before. All un-Godly habits were left in Pittsburg and a
new life was waiting for me in Arizona. A new life waiting is waiting
for all of you reading this book. Just don't take the old baggage with
you. Let God do a new thing in your life. Arizona was a beautiful
place, a paradise, palm trees, sun and fun! Arizona was the cleanest
place I had ever been. It's just hot, I mean real hot. I mean hell hot.
During my first season, in 1991, the temperature was 126 degrees and

we were playing football. How did we do that? Just thinking about it now is crazy! You can do anything if you put your all into it!

My coaches were Pete Rodriquez for Special Teams, Mike Murphy was my inside linebacker positon coach and Ted Cottrell was defensive line coach. I loved Coach Rodriquez's excitement and Coach Murphy was a great guy. Coach Ted Cotrell was my College coach at Rutgers! I could remember the day he came to my house with big cowboy boots on. Our defensive back coach was Jimmy Johnson! Fitz Sherman was our defensive co-ordinate, and our Head Coach was Joe Bugle! I loved Coach Bugle. He was an old school coach and it was all about the basics- hitting, tackling, running, blocking, passing, and catching! We had a good nucleolus for a team and our quarterback at that time was Tim Rosenbal. We also had Chris Chandler, Tom Tupa, and Stan Gelbaugh. As Running Back, we had John Johnson and he was the man. Larry Centers was hustling his way on the field. He was a future Pro Bowler, and I witnessed his maturity to become a great player. At the wide receiver positions were Rickey Proehl & Ernie Jones. On the defensive side of the ball, we had some good players as well. Leading the way was "T Mack" Tim McDonald. He was a Pro Bowler and a great player for us. Next was the Big Boy, Eric Hill, "E. Hill" from LSU. He too was the man along with Freddie Joe, Nunn and Ken Harvey. In the secondary were Mike "Z-man" Zordich, Robert Massey, Lorenzo Lynch, and, saving the best for last, Aeneas "The Work Horse" Williams. Aeneas was also an All Pro in the making, with multiple All Pro selections. Aeneas was one of the most committed players I have ever seen. He was younger than me, yet more mature naturally and spiritually and we are great friends to this day.

<u>Cracking the Starting line up!</u>

At about mid-season, we had a losing record and the defense was not giving Coach Fritz what he wanted. Coach Fritz threw me in against the Dallas Cowboys and for the next two and a half years, I started as inside linebacker for the Arizona Cardinals! I signed a new contract and made some real money. I'm a Cardinals Fan for life.

To the Bidwill family and to the Arizona Cardinals organization, I thank you for allowing me to reach my dream's potential and for trusting me enough with a chance at the starting job!

Our 1993 season was exciting, we made great strides and finished with a strong record! We were poised to use that momentum to have a winning season and save Joe Bugle from losing his job! But we didn't have some of our key players get signed and other went to different teams. Two of our good player that wasn't signed were Eric Hill and Robert Massey.

ASSOCIATED PRESS
Cardinals' Tyronne Stowe, right, a Passaic native, moving in to tackle Giants' Rodney Hampton on Sunday, as Jeff Faulkner gets blocked.

Tyronne Stowe tackling Rodney Hampton

They were key people to our defensive success. That season we had improved greatly, but came short of having a winning season. We ended the year with a record of 7-9. We came up short and Coach Joe bugle was fired. Eric Hill was missing, Robert Massey was missing on the defensive side, and those two pieces meant a lot to us! That season, even though we had a record, in the end, we came up short, and Coach Joe Bugle was fired.

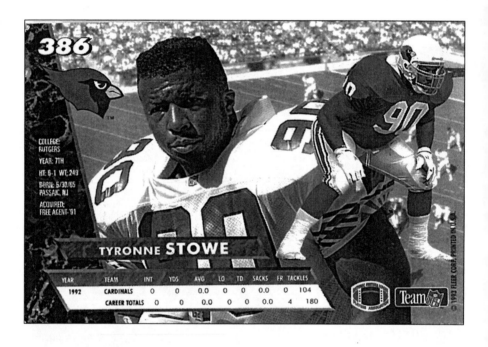

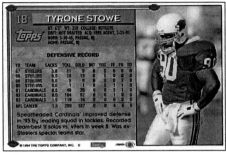

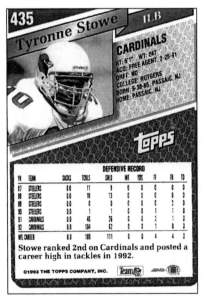

3 Cardinal cards front and back two other card front and back, (22,23) (24, 25)

Chapter 17

A WINNER IS IN TOWN!

After breaking the starting lineup and three seasons with the Phoenix Cardinals, Coach Joe Bugle was fired and we just missed having a .500 season, which was an improvement from the past. As a result, our key players were not signed and it caused us not to get off to a good start. The new coach was named Buddy Ryan, who came in and claimed a winner was in town. Buddy was just that too, he had won in Chicago and Philadelphia! The question was; how would the winner fair in Arizona? When Buddy came in, so did his people. Buddy was a man that was going to do it his way, which is something that I admire about him. If you are going to do anything, you should come in and go out singing like Frank Sinatra. I did it my way! Buddy came in and I was traded out. The 46 defense was Buddy signet invention. He was a great defensive mind. The 46 defense attacked the offense. You would call the defenses based off the offense sets, predicted the defense ran. Man to man cover was my weak point, remember I was the slow train and I didn't fit the winner playing scheme, and I was not included, the undrafted free agent that was cut twice, scab player that crossed the line, broke into the starting lineup was traded to the Washington Redskins for a third round draft pick!

Do you understand what is happening as you keep pursuing the dream? You are developing, growing, and maturing. More value is being added unto you, your stock is rising and your appraisal is increased. It took me seven years to be worthy of a third round draft pick! Prove all your critics wrong and show them who you really are. Can I tell you there is more to you than what they can see? Go forth and show them who you really are. It's already in you, even when they didn't pick you, you had it. Some people will not see your intrinsic value but as long as you know that there is an MVP in you, be a star in your own show. Show the world what you have, or as the young folks would say, "show em what you working with!"

Traded

The team that I love now didn't want me anymore and I felt abandoned. I understood it was business, but I didn't want to go, and I knew I couldn't stay. Sometimes we have to do what you have to do and sometimes you have to leave. Leave the old to get with the new! It's something to be learned in everything. Don't stay in situations where you are not wanted! Find a place where you fit and this trade, put me back in a place of uncertainty. I was in a new place, on a new team, with a new Coach with a new quarterback. Change is sometimes not easy to deal with. I had to start all over again proving myself and making the team again. I had to start all over again and prove myself and make the team again!

Coach Nor Turner was the Head Coach

I started for the Washington Redskins that year, things were different from what I was used to and I couldn't get comfortable. I couldn't find my groove, and had an ok year, but the defense wasn't the problem.

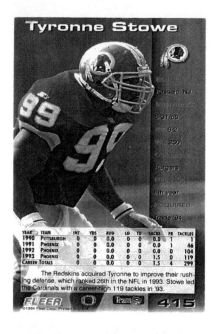

Tyronne Stowe

Passaic, NJ

5-31-65

6-2

250

Rutgers

6th year

ACQUIRED
Trade '94

YEAR	TEAM	INT	YDS	AVG	LG	TD	SACKS	FR	TACKLES
1990	PITTSBURGH	0	0	0.0	0	0	0.0	1	1
1991	PHOENIX	0	0	0.0	0	0	0.0	1	46
1992	PHOENIX	0	0	0.0	0	0	0.0	0	104
1993	PHOENIX	0	0	0.0	0	0	1.5	0	119
CAREER TOTALS		0	0	0.0	0	0	1.5	4	299

The Redskins acquired Tyronne to improve their rushing defense, which ranked 26th in the NFL in 1993. Stowe led the Cardinals with a career-high 119 tackles in '93.

FLEER
©1994 Fleer Corp.

Team

415

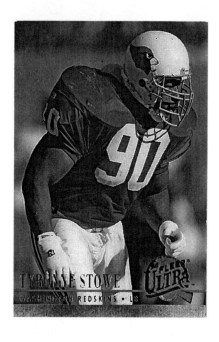

TYRONNE STOWE

WASHINGTON REDSKINS • LB

FLEER ULTRA

TYRONNE STOWE

GAMEDAY '93
THE OFFICIAL NFL CARD

Tyronne Stowe
HT: 6'2" WT: 250 COLLEGE: RUTGERS
DFT: NOT DRAFTED ACQ: TRADE WITH CARDINALS, 6-17-94
BORN: 5-30-65, PASSAIC, NJ HOME: PASSAIC, NJ

		DEFENSIVE RECORD						
YR	TEAM	SACKS	TCKL	SOLO	INT	YDS	FF	FR	TD
87	STEELERS	0.0	11	9	0	0	0	0	0
88	STEELERS	0.0	18	13	0	0	0	0	0
89	STEELERS	0.0	0	0	0	0	2	0	0
90	STEELERS	0.0	1	1	0	0	1	1	0
91	CARDINALS	0.0	46	28	0	0	2	1	0
92	CARDINALS	0.0	104	62	0	0	1	0	0
93	CARDINALS	1.5	119	78	0	0	0	0	0
94	REDSKINS	0.0	157	80	1	2	1	0	0
NFL CAREER		1.5	456	267	1	2	5	4	0

Impact player who helped 'Skins defend run. Acquired in trade with Cardinals. Second on team in tackles. Hustler who chipped in on special teams. Once blocked for Craig "Ironhead" Heyward in high school.

© 1994 THE TOPPS COMPANY, INC.

team   PLAYERS   51

102

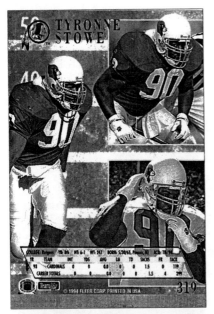

I'm happy to say, our number one pick, Quarterback was Heath Shula and is one of our representatives in Washington now! His rookie year was not nice to us, as I can remember people cursing him out and running unto the field after he threw another interception.

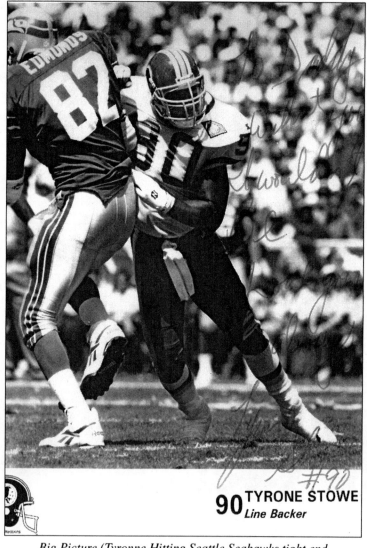

Big Picture (Tyronne Hitting Seattle Seahawks tight end # 82 Ferrell Edmonds).

Health Shula threw 14 interceptions or so. We only played 16 games. Almost one a game it's hard to win like that and my one-year tenure with the Redskins was up.

I got released, again I felt like a three times. I felt like I had struck out. I was second on the team in tackles behind Andrea Collins and they cut me and kept Shula. I got released, again and felt like a three time looser. How many times have you gotten fired? How many times have doors been shut in your face? How many times, has your dream been cut? Just keep enduring until the end! Proverbs 24:16 "For a righteous man falls seven times, and rises again"

Chapter 18

SLEEPLESS IN SEATTLE

Coach Mike Murphy, the Linebacker Coach with the Cardinals, was now with the Seattle Seahawks! I had just got released by the Washington Redskins and Seattle called me! I'm rising again, yet I was tired of the roller coaster ride. Not sure what was next. I got a call that a deal was done for me! A one-year deal to prove my worth and the opportunity to compete for the starting job! I had to start all over again, prove myself, but I won the starting job at inside linebacker. I was leading the team in tackles.

About the eighth game of the season, we were playing in Buffalo, against Jim Kelly and the Bills. I could remember tackling Thurmon Thomas and experienced a slight pain in my right forearm. I was not sure, what it was but I know it didn't feel right. I stayed in one more play only to run to the side line to get it checked out. The doctor was not sure but they said something was wrong. After getting an x ray, they found out I had broken my right forearm!

Broken Dreams

I was left alone in Seattle, my wife and children were in Phoenix and I encountered many nights, sleepless in Seattle. I found myself battling to stay positive through this bad break. The team was preparing for the rest of the season, and I was done for the season! The gray clouds of Seattle were settling in on me. I couldn't sleep or eat. I returned home to Arizona to complete my rehab, and I was in a cast for four months, thinking that a clean break would fuse back together!

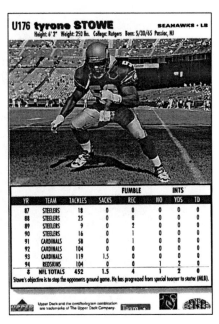

U176 **tyrone STOWE**   SEAHAWKS • LB
Height: 6' 2" Weight: 250 lbs. College: Rutgers Born: 5/30/65 Passaic, NJ

YR	TEAM	TACKLES	SACKS	FUMBLE REC	NO	INTS YDS	TD
87	STEELERS	18	0	0	0	0	0
88	STEELERS	25	0	0	0	0	0
89	STEELERS	9	0	2	0	0	0
90	STEELERS	16	0	1	0	0	0
91	CARDINALS	58	0	1	0	0	0
92	CARDINALS	104	0	0	0	0	0
93	CARDINALS	119	1.5	0	0	0	0
94	REDSKINS	104	0	0	1	2	0
8	NFL TOTALS	452	1.5	4	1	2	0

Stowe's objective is to stop the opponents ground game. He has progressed from special teamer to starter (MLB).

tyrone
Seattle SEAHAWKS • LB

The break did not fuse back together and I lost four months of rehab. They had to do surgery on my forearm and insert eight screws. This lost time was critical for my recovery. Once pre-season started, I broke it again and I was forced to retire because of my injuries. The dream was over I could no longer play the game I loved.

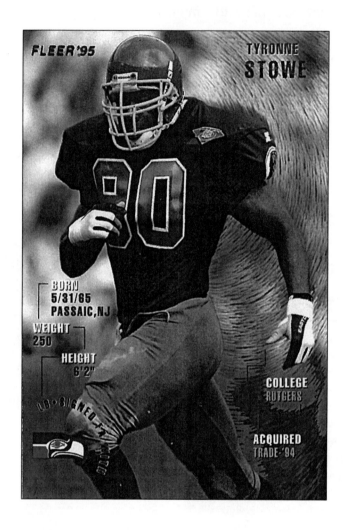

Chapter 19

THE NFL EXPERIENCE

Looking back and reflecting on my remarkable NFL career, all I can say is I did it my way. Yes, I would have done some things differently and I would have loved to end this story with Super Bowl Rings, money, fortune and fame, MVP or all pro Status, but that wasn't what I wanted, that's not what I asked for. You have to be very careful for what you ask for, you might just get it! I want to close with thanking the NFL for the experience of a life time. No one can mark the master piece of a dream that was carved out of nothing. God has truly blessed me to see the value in life. I pray, you have gained new energy and determination to support your dream and make it your reality. Don't look back later in life, wishing that you would have done it. Do it now, while you have time, while the window of opportunity is open, while it's still in your mind. The dream will take you places and introduce you to great people. Proverbs 18:16 "A gift opens the way and ushers the giver into the presence of the great."

Football gave me the opportunity to travel all across America playing my childhood game. When Life is all said and done, will you be able to say, "I did it my way". I lived my dream! The Pro Scouts, and Coaches didn't think I could do it, and ten years on the grid iron I held a job that has yielded me a life full of memories. I still feel like a fish out of water but time has moved on and I know that I'm not able to do this anymore. I miss the fellowship and comradery of the boys getting together as teammates. The NFL experience has taught me, to never stop believing in myself.

My body is pain ridden, my back and my neck are daily reminders that I did it. I paid the price for success, and no-one can ever take that away from me. It took great strength to get me this far. I had to exert the inner power for me to transform my life into what I wanted it to be. This journey has been a fight, and has made me a stronger man, by staying fixated on a dream that I wanted! Yes, I wanted it bad enough, to go through the ups and downs of life. A private joke for the NFL Not for Long, as the average career is three to four years and I played 10 special years I am receiving a check for doing a job they said I wasn't good enough to do. The dream has yielded memories and lessons of a life time. I want to sum it up this way; your window of opportunities are closing, it's time for you to live your dream. Retired now, and looking back at some wonder lessons I've learned that all the obstacles I had to overcome to be a part of an elite group of athletes that every boy dreamed about, but I can surely say "I did it!" Hopefully as you have read the book something inside you was ignited for you to do it too! Each day get up answering your critics, I want it bad enough! Don't worry about what they say, all that matters is what you say every day. Work on your dream and it will work for you! I've had a great life living the dream! Now it your turn! May the Lord bless you, and keep you; The Lord make His face shine on you,

And be gracious to you;

The LORD lift up His countenance on you, And give you peace.'

Numbers 6:24-26

CPSIA information can be obtained
at www.ICGtesting.com
Printed in the USA
BVOW00s0434221216
471563BV00003B/6/P